Stones from the River of Mercy

STONES FROM THE

River of Mercy

A SPIRITUAL JOURNAL

Sheila Walsh

A
JANET
THOMA
BOOK

THOMAS NELSON PUBLISHERS
Nashville

Published in Nashville, Tennessee, by Thomas Nelson, Inc.

Scripture quotations noted NKJV are from THE NEW KING JAMES VERSION. Copyright © 1979, 1980, 1982, Thomas Nelson, Inc., Publishers.

Scripture quotations noted NASB are from the NEW AMERICAN STANDARD BIBLE®, Copyright © The Lockman Foundation 1960, 1962, 1963, 1968, 1971, 1972, 1973, 1975, 1977. Used by permission.

Scripture quotations noted NIV are from the HOLY BIBLE: NEW INTERNATIONAL VERSION®. Copyright © 1973, 1978, 1984 by International Bible Society. Used by permission of Zondervan Publishing House. All rights reserved.

ISBN: 978-1-4002-7796-4

Printed in the United States of America
1 2 3 4 5 6 7 8 9 10 HART 09 08 07 06 05 04 03 02 01 00

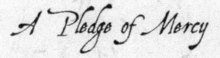

A Pledge of Mercy

I want to leave a brighter trail for those who come behind.

I want to be a candle burning in the darkest night.

I want to be a shoulder strong enough for crying on.

I want to walk with those whose shoes are worn.

I want to tell the smallest child, "Look up. You're not alone."

I want to take the oldest face and hold it to my own.

I want to sing from every hill and shout from every wall,

"Because He lives, there's mercy for us all."

Contents

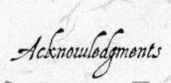

Acknowledgments

Special thanks to Melanee Bandy, Connie Reece, and Anne Trudel
for the care, time, and hard work
they put into this journal.
My heartfelt thanks to my editor, Janet Thoma,
who always gives more
than I could hope or ask for.

*M*y husband, Barry, and I are members of Christ Presbyterian Church, a church of about twenty-five hundred members here in Nashville. The small group we belong to meets every Sunday night. They are an unusual group of people, drawn together by their zany ways and slight irreverence.

Because I travel so much with Women of Faith, we often miss Sunday morning worship, but we are often back in time for Sunday night. Ours is the kind of group where if you come and you are tired—if Barry is in a T-shirt and I'm in a ball cap—you can drag yourself in and just sit there. You don't have to contribute anything or try to be something you're not. Other members bring you a cup of coffee and love on you. Even though we meet on Sunday nights, we also include the children, so Christian, our son, can participate.

At the end of 1998, one of the couples who had been praying for a child for a long time gave birth to a little girl. Hope was a darling little baby, but within the first two weeks of her life, the parents found out she had a very rare disease. Most children with this disease do not live beyond their first birthday.

In the spring of 1999, our small group decided to have a big bash at Percy Warner Park, a large park in Nashville, to celebrate Hope's six-month birthday; we knew she probably wouldn't live to have a full-year birthday.

Balloons were everywhere. All the children came, and little Hope, in her father's arms, was the guest of honor.

Most of us had come from church, and we had pretty decent clothes on. About mid-afternoon our pastor came over to me and said, "Look at your son! He got hold of the hose and found a five-year-old who was willing to turn it on for him."

Christian, in his gorgeous white linen suit and white leather shoes, was hosing everyone in sight. He was drenched from top to bottom, as were several others. I ran over to rescue everybody, and Christian turned the hose on me. We all laughed and had a great day, an unexpected grace amidst a broken dream.

One week later Hope went home to be with the Lord.

I cannot imagine burying a child. It was difficult to watch Barry losing his mother, Eleanor, in the spring of 1999. But a parent burying a child—that's not the way it is supposed to be! One of the things that makes it possible for Christians to bear the unbearable is that we bring Christ to one another. We are called to be in community.

Through Eleanor's and Hope's deaths, I came to realize that in our best moments we live in the grace and mercy and love of God. And during this last year I have been searching the Scriptures to learn more about God's grace and mercy. In this book you accompany me in that journey.

Now I think God is calling me to live with a sense of grief for the brokenness of the world and to intercede for people all around me. It's a call for me to grow up. To stop being the child. To become the Father's instrument.

Barry said to me the other day, "I didn't want my mother to die. I still want to be the little boy; I don't want to be the grownup." We all feel that way. But there is a call these days to stop being the child, to receive God's grace, and then become the Father who is waiting for the prodigal son with arms open wide and a tear-stained face.

During the Women of Faith Conference in Detroit, Christian was up all Thursday night with a fever, and I had to speak on Friday. I had just gone through all the trauma of the funeral and my father-in-law moving in with us, and I was so tired.

Yet I held Christian and sat with him until about five in the morning. Obviously, as a mother, that's what you do. This new spiritual calling in my life becomes so clear to me as I mother my son, because children expect to receive. That's why a mother and father are there. Someday if Christian becomes a father, he will have to put aside his own needs for the sake of his child.

I understand my physical life as a mother clearly: It's time to put aside my own needs and be there for my son. The parallel in my spiritual life is to grow up and be there for other people with open arms, to be the one who will give out the grace and the mercy of God.

This book is meant to be a journey in finding this courage and strength. I have called the book *Stones from the River of Mercy* because of a little-known passage in Joshua, chapters 3 and 4. On their trek to the promised land, the people of Israel needed to cross the huge Jordan River—about twenty yards wide, deeper than a man's height, with a current so strong, it is impossible to cross at the time of its overflowing in the spring. Yet God had the solution. He supernaturally held up the waters from the riverbed, allowing the whole nation to cross safely on dry ground.

But God did not want the Israelites to forget this event, so He instructed them to carry with them stones from the river—tangible objects—to remind themselves and

to serve as a teaching tool for future generations. He also told them to construct a monument there, in the middle of the Jordan, for the same purpose.

The men carried twelve stones from the riverbed to Gilgal, at the eastern edge of the city of Jericho, where they camped for the night and constructed a monument. Then, when future generations asked about this edifice, their parents could tell them, "It is to remind us that the Jordan River stopped flowing when the Ark of God went across!"

I believe God also intends for us to hold onto moments in our lives, to build memories of times when we received His mercy and grace in deep blue waters. Then, when we again face trauma, we can say to ourselves, *God helped me through these times in the past. He'll walk with me now.*

This journal is meant to be a book of remembrance and growth. At the same time that we look at Scriptures to learn about God's mercy and grace, you will also have the opportunity to record your personal stories of His mercy during that week.

At Women of Faith Conferences, many women stand in line to speak to me. I know they are interested in hearing more of my story, but I also know they want to share their own stories. This journal offers each of us the opportunity to record moments of God's mercy in our lives.

If you feel inspired to share one of your stories with me, please feel free to write me:

Sheila Walsh
P.O. Box 150783
Nashville, TN 37215

Let me know if you would be willing for me to share your story when I speak or write a future book.

Stones from the River of Mercy is also meant to be a personal reflection of your journey with the Lord. You might want to save this journal and reread it later. Or share it with a daughter or sister in Christ.

Throughout this book we will look at different aspects of God's mercy and grace. Technically, these words have subtle shades of meaning that can distinguish them from each other. But in this journal, I am using the two interchangeably, referring to the whole of the concept.

The Bible also seems to use these two terms in this way. You can see this in the parallel form of Hebrew poetry, in which one line states a fact, and the following line restates it in slightly different wording. One line will use *gracious*; the next will use *merciful*, trying to get across the same idea.

In Weeks 1 through 3 of the journal, we will look at Scriptures that reveal the different aspects of God's grace and mercy: It's new every morning, it's sufficient for suffering, and it's paradoxical. In later weeks we will look at the character of our graceful God: His love, His kindness, His justice, and His patience. And then we will see how the Scriptures tell us to receive God's grace and respond to it by living out the Kingdom principle of giving and receiving.

Each day focuses on a particular Scripture, which will provide the inspiration to help you relate that passage to your daily journey. You might want to refer to the entire chapter in the Bible before you journal. If not, I have summarized the context for you. And if the Scripture inspires you to write something different than the questions at the end of the passage suggest, please feel free to do so. This journal is meant to be *your* journey into a deeper relationship with the Lord because of your new appreciation for His grace and mercy.

Throughout the book are stories of God's love and mercy, some from interviews I conducted when I was the cohost of *The 700 Club*, and some from letters from friends and women who've attended Women of Faith Conferences.

This journal, the book *Stories from the River of Mercy*, and my album *Blue Waters* are meant to be a blessed journey toward our Savior. Read *Stories from the River of Mercy* to see God's love and grace to Eleanor and me in deep blue waters. Use this journal to hear God's promises of grace in the Bible and apply them to your own life. And then listen to the songs on the album *Blue Waters* and sing God's mercy into your own life. My hope is that you, too, will be changed as you are plunged into God's river of mercy.

An Eye-Opening Experience:

Getting to Know Aspects of God's Grace and Mercy

*M*ost of us tend to think of God's grace and mercy as part of a broad, somewhat vague concept. And though we know that concept is a good thing, it has little practical meaning to us. But reading the numerous Scriptures that refer to God's grace and mercy can be a real eye-opening experience. Each verse sheds a little more light on all its many parts; when you look more closely, you start to see intricate facets you wouldn't have noticed at first glance. It is almost surprising, yet exciting, to realize the fullness and depth of God's mercy.

You will spend the next three weeks poring over a few of the many details that make up the whole of God's grace and mercy. Take your time and enjoy getting to know more fully what God's grace and mercy really mean.

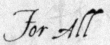

I am not ashamed of the gospel, because it is the power of God for the salvation of everyone who believes: first for the Jew, then for the Gentile.

Romans 1:16 NIV

Paul's beginning statement in Romans sets the theme for his entire letter. What better way is there to begin a discussion of God's grace than to point out that it is available to all? God's mercy is so great that He is *compelled* to offer it to everyone. Many have heard about it but choose not to partake. But as hard as it is to believe, there are still people who are either unaware of this great gift or unaware that it is available to them personally.

*W*rite about the part you can play in helping others learn about God's mercy and grace.

_____

_____

_____

_____

_____

_____

_____

*M*y Prayer for This Day:

_____

_____

_____

_____

_____

Motivated by Love

For God so loved the world that He gave His only begotten Son, that whoever believes in Him should not perish but have everlasting life.

John 3:16 NKJV

In these familiar words to Nicodemus, Jesus revealed God's sole motivation in making salvation available to a world of sinners bound for eternal death. Only a love beyond the scope of our imagination would motivate such an extension of mercy at such a high cost to the Giver—God's sacrifice of His only Son in exchange for our eternal lives.

Describe an opportunity right now in your life to follow God's example and to make a sacrifice motivated by love.

_____

_____

_____

_____

_____

_____

_____

_____

My Prayer for This Day:

_____

_____

_____

_____

_____

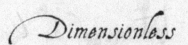

For Your mercy reaches unto the heavens,
And Your truth unto the clouds.

Psalm 57:10 NKJV

David wrote this psalm while he was hiding from Saul, who was out to kill him. How appropriate it was for David to be considering the vast reaches of God's mercy as he hid in the depths of a cave. The mercy of the Most High God can't be held in by traditional boundaries—the earth itself cannot contain it all. In fact, it often reaches into places—and to people—in ways we could not have predicted.

*N*ame a person you know who once was so far from God that you thought he or she could never change. Describe the difference once God's mercy touched him or her.

_____

_____

_____

_____

_____

_____

_____

_____

*M*y Prayer for This Day:

_____

_____

_____

_____

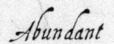

And the grace of our Lord was exceedingly abundant.
1 Timothy 1:14 NKJV

As Paul wrote to Timothy about the contrast between his life before and after Christ, he couldn't help but stop and acknowledge the abundance of God's grace, which he had experienced not only at conversion but also later in his ministry. God's grace is abundant in many ways. It is abundant by nature—before we ever receive it; it is permanently a part of the person of God, and His mercy is always great. But God's grace is also abundant as we receive it. God often surprises us with the generous portions of mercy He supplies at just the right moments.

*R*evisit a moment from your life in which the abundance of God's mercy flowed generously at just the right time.

_____

_____

_____

_____

_____

_____

*M*y Prayer for This Day:

_____

_____

_____

_____

_____

But the free gift is not like the transgression. For if by the transgression of the one the many died, much more did the grace of God and the gift by the grace of the one Man, Jesus Christ, abound to the many.

Romans 5:15 NASB

In this passage in Romans, Paul was establishing the fact that nothing compares to God's gracious gift of Jesus. Any gift is given at the cost of the giver. The receiver has no obligation for the price the giver has already paid. If the price of the gift of salvation has already been paid, as God says it has been through Christ, what more is left for you to do than to respond with gratitude as any gift-receiver would?

Detail five ways you personally can live out your gratitude for God's free gift of grace.

_____

_____

_____

_____

_____

_____

_____

My Prayer for This Day:

_____

_____

_____

_____

_____

Reflect back on this week's topic: the aspects of God's grace and mercy, given . . .

- for us all
- motivated by love
- without dimension
- abundantly
- freely

. . . by God, your Father.

*N*ow write your personal story of God's mercy to you this week.

_____

_____

_____

_____

_____

_____

_____

_____

_____

_____

_____

_____

_____

_____

An Inch from the Gates of Hell

*W*hen I was sixteen years old, I asked the headmaster of my school if I could show the movie *The Cross and the Switchblade* at lunchtime to all sixteen hundred students. I was excited when he gave me permission. I was the only Christian that I knew of in the student body, and I felt that the story of this film would change lives.

The day we showed the movie, the auditorium was packed. As the story began to unfold, you could have heard a pin drop. Unfortunately, I had never seen anyone inject themselves with drugs, so when it got to that part, I fainted and was carried out by Mr. Lunam, the biology teacher!

Years later I met Nicky Cruz, the main character of the movie, when I interviewed him. Nicky was the eighth son in a Puerto Rican family that practiced black magic and witchcraft. His parents believed in good and bad demonic spirits and felt that they were in touch with the good ones. His father, Yelo Cruz, called "the Great One," was a rural healer who communicated with powerful spirits. He expected Nicky to follow in his footsteps.

As a two-month-old baby, Nicky nearly died of a strange fever. Torn with grief, his father took his wife's best black hen and began to chant and cast a spell. Suddenly, he chopped off the hen's head and let the blood spill over his son. Nicky lived. But his mother began to believe that Nicky was evil. When he was eight years old, she told him she hated him. "You have been cursed from the day you were born," she said. "You are not my son; you are the son of Satan." Nicky lost all feeling that day—he never cried again during his childhood.

When Nicky was fifteen years old, his father took him to the airport, gave him a ten-dollar bill and a plane ticket to New York, and wished him a better life. In New York, Nicky fell in with a street gang called the Mau Maus, and he continued his life of violence and hatred. Often as he lay in bed at night, though thousands of miles away from his home, he was still haunted by his mother's words: "You are the son of Satan."

One day a skinny preacher walked up to Nicky, looked him straight in the eyes, and said, "Nicky, Jesus loves you." Nicky was enraged. No one loved him—no one had ever loved him. He determined to kill the preacher, but there was something about this man

that he couldn't fight. Nicky went to an evening church service with a gun in his pocket, bent on blowing David Wilkerson away. When David saw Nicky enter the church, he began to pray aloud for Nicky. God melted Nicky's heart, and he began to cry out to God to forgive him. For the first time in his life, he knew he was loved—he wasn't a mistake. He began working on the streets with Dave, sharing his new life with friends and rival gang members.

Nicky's brother Frank, who was also living in New York, bumped into Nicky one day. "Mama's searching for you. She's dying, Nicky," said Frank. Bitterness and hatred toward this woman who had cursed him overwhelmed Nicky. But he knew in his heart that he had to forgive her. He flew home to Puerto Rico, apprehensive about the spiritual battle ahead. His father and brothers met him at the airport—they were friendly but distant, trying to sense if his power was greater than theirs. When Nicky saw his mother, he was shocked. She was old, thin, and deathly ill.

Nicky escaped from the house for a while and made his way to the local church, where the congregation had met for prayer. He asked the pastor to bring some other believers to his house that night and pray for his mother. "I'll never enter that evil-spirited house," a church member cried out. But the pastor understood and agreed to come.

Nicky bought his mother a new dress that afternoon and took it home to her. He helped her put on the dress and then washed her face and combed her hair. He carried her to the living room sofa, and as they sat there, he heard a noise outside. Nicky rushed to the window and saw five hundred Christians coming toward the house with guitars and tambourines, singing the praise of Jesus. Nicky's father slipped away and hid in the forest behind the house. But that night Nicky's mom was gloriously saved and healed. She lived for another twenty-five years!

When Nicky's father was almost eighty years old, he lay in a hospital, weak and afraid. "All my life I have served lying and deceiving spirits. If I try to call on the name of the Lord now, they will kill me." Nicky assured his father that the One he loved and served is greater and stronger than the one who is in the world. He told him not to be afraid.

Finally, one day, Yelo Cruz told his son, "I've made my choice. I'm going to give my life to Jesus and I'm going to ask Him to take me then." Nicky's father prayed a simple, fervent prayer, and a glorious peace illuminated his face. Eight hours later, he died. He found salvation at the very gates of hell.

Nicky told me that he often wonders what kind of man his father would have been if he had met Christ as a young man. Yelo Cruz wasted his life in the service of the destroyer. In his last days, the powers he had served all his life turned on him; yet Yelo discovered the truth those who love Jesus know: When God's Spirit is in you, the very gates of hell cannot prevail against you.

This Week's Praises, Petitions, and Intercessions

*R*eserve this page for any petitions for yourself or intercessions for others that have come to your mind and heart as you journal this week. Go to God in prayer and record how and when He answers you. Praise Him for His tender, loving care.

PETITIONS

ANSWERS

_____

_____

_____

_____

_____

_____

_____

_____

_____

INTERCESSIONS

ANSWERS

_____

_____

_____

_____

_____

_____

_____

_____

_____

And God is able to make all grace abound toward you, that you, always having all sufficiency in all things, may have an abundance for every good work.

2 Corinthians 9:8 NKJV

In his letter to the Corinthians, Paul made an important point about the enabling power of grace in the context of its direct relation to giving—the more you give, either in sum or deed, the more God will give you, so you can continue to be generous. In other words, give liberally, and God's grace will continue to enable you—don't worry about your supply running low.

Consider carefully your attitude toward giving. What hinders you from giving more?

_____

_____

_____

_____

Write how you plan to let God's grace enable you to give more freely and generously.

_____

_____

_____

_____

My Prayer for This Day:

_____

_____

_____

_____

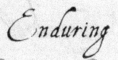
> *Oh, give thanks to the LORD, for He is good!*
> *For His mercy endures forever.*
>
> Psalm 136:1 NKJV

This verse comes right at the beginning of a psalm that recounts God's lengthy and consistent history with the Israelite nation. Starting with creation, the psalmist listed God's acts of mercy, then repeatedly proclaimed the enduring quality of God's mercy. God's enduring, continued mercy to the Israelites is evidence of how He responds to His spiritual Israel, the Church.

*L*ook back over your history with God. List His acts of mercy toward you personally.

_____

_____

_____

_____

_____

_____

_____

_____

*M*y Prayer for This Day:

_____

_____

_____

_____

_____

. . . according to the power of God, who has saved us and called us with a holy calling . . . according to His own purpose and grace which was given to us in Christ Jesus before time began.

2 Timothy 1:8-9 NKJV

Encouraging the young Timothy in his ministry, Paul made it clear that God's grace is not just a generous gesture—it is full of purpose. God's general purpose is for man to be reconciled (made right) with Him. But God has a specific purpose for each one of us who has been reconciled, and, not surprisingly, that purpose works to carry out His general purpose.

*R*elate what you sense is God's purpose for you personally, keeping in mind His general purpose for man.

_____

_____

_____

_____

_____

_____

_____

*M*y Prayer for This Day:

_____

_____

_____

_____

_____

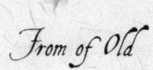

> *Remember, O LORD, Your tender mercies and Your*
> *lovingkindnesses,*
> *For they are from of old.*
>
> Psalm 25:6 NKJV

In this psalm of instruction, David points out the timeless nature of God's mercy. Indeed, God's mercy has proved itself through the ages. People from all centuries have experienced it, and we have that in common with them.

*R*eflect on how God has used history—people and events from years before—to bring the message of His ageless mercy to you.

*P*eople

_____

_____

_____

*E*vents

_____

_____

_____

*M*y Prayer for This Day:

_____

_____

_____

_____

_____

Through the LORD's mercies we are not consumed . . .
They are new every morning.

Lamentations 3:22–23 NKJV

In a book that was written as a funeral dirge mourning the destruction of Jerusalem and the sin that led to it, the prophet Jeremiah paused in his despair to praise God for His great mercy. It is during the dark times—whether caused by our own sin or not—that we feel we must have exhausted God's supply of mercy. But, as Jeremiah was keenly aware, God gives us fresh mercy every morning—enough to get through one day at a time.

*W*rite about the new mercy God supplied for you this morning for your situation.

_____

_____

_____

_____

_____

_____

_____

*M*y Prayer for This Day:

_____

_____

_____

_____

_____

Reflect on this week's topic: the aspects of God's grace and mercy, which are . . .

* enabling
* enduring
* purposeful
* from of old
* new every morning

*N*ow write your personal story of God's mercy to you this week.

_____

_____

_____

_____

_____

_____

_____

_____

_____

_____

_____

_____

_____

_____

_____

A Story of God's Mercy

Out of the Abyss

I am always blessed when I receive a letter from someone who has experienced God's mercy. Here is the experience of Jean from Wisconsin:

We've often heard people say, "God works in mysterious ways." That truth became a reality in my life when I was thrown into the abyss of clinical depression.

I have been called to be an elementary teacher, the mother of two beautiful daughters, and the wife to a compassionate husband. Over a period of a few years, I was overcome by my own expectations, my own fears, my own guilt, and my own shame. I was increasingly irritable, fatigued, and anxious. I seemed to be a stranger in my own world. When my thoughts of escape eventually turned to leaving this world, I knew I needed help. I then began a dark, agonizing climb out of the abyss of depression.

One Sunday morning I tuned into *The Hour of Power* with Robert Schuller and heard you speak of your own experiences with depression. I felt as if you were talking to me.

I realized I was not alone in my battles, and I bought your book *Honestly*, which filled me with a sense of hope and strength to continue my climb. Within a week I got a pamphlet for the 1997 Women of Faith Conferences, and you were listed as a speaker. I felt the compelling voice of the Holy Spirit urging me to go. I knew the Lord was showing me a way out of my dark hole. He was preparing me to open my heart to His grace and unconditional love.

As I listened to the conference speakers, I came to terms with the reality of my life—past and present. I had always felt that somehow I was to blame for the way others treated me. A deep sense of guilt, responsibility, and perfectionism was instilled in me. I felt that love was to be earned and that I never quite did enough, or was good enough, to be truly loved.

Now I know that it was others in my life who wronged me, not I who wronged them. I was finally able to free myself of my guilt and shame and accept the unconditional love our Lord has to offer. I gained new hope for my future and renewed my relationships with my Lord, my family, and my friends.

Now, one year later, my husband and I are closer than ever. We will continue to face

the challenge of keeping my depression under control. Still, the Lord has answered our prayers by providing people to uphold us and support us. He has put His arms around us like a warm blanket in a cold, dark rain.

The Women of Faith have reminded me that life is tough, but God is faithful. His ways are mysterious, but His love and grace are endless. I have come to realize that God answers prayer not with bolts of lightning, but by providing the right people, the right medication, and the right words—at just the right time.

Miracles happen all around us—in people's everyday lives. We just need to open our eyes and hearts. If life becomes overwhelming and I feel as if I'm treading water in a stormy ocean, fighting to survive, I now know that God can be the life jacket to keep my head above the deep blue waters.

This Week's Praises, Petitions, and Intercessions

$\mathcal{R}$eserve this page for any petitions for yourself or intercessions for others that have come to your mind and heart as you journal this week. Go to God in prayer and record how and when He answers you. Praise Him for His tender, loving care.

PETITIONS

ANSWERS

_____

_____

_____

_____

_____

_____

_____

_____

INTERCESSIONS

ANSWERS

_____

_____

_____

_____

_____

_____

_____

_____

For by grace you have been saved through faith, and that not of yourselves; it is the gift of God.

Ephesians 2:8 NKJV

In an effort to help the Ephesians understand who they were in Christ, Paul reminded them that they indeed were saved, but they had made no contribution to their own salvation; Christ had already accomplished it for them. What God did through Jesus on the cross was not only an incomparable act of grace, it was sufficient—all that was needed— for all people for all time.

*R*ead Hebrews 10:12. Then write about the finality of Christ's sacrifice and our lack of both need and ability to add to it.

_____

_____

_____

_____

_____

_____

_____

_____

*M*y Prayer for This Day:

_____

_____

_____

_____

Sufficient for Suffering

Concerning this thing I pleaded with the Lord three times that it might depart from me. And He said to me, "My grace is sufficient for you, for My strength is made perfect in weakness."

2 Corinthians 12:8–9 NKJV

After describing to the Corinthians a heavenly vision God had given him, Paul balanced that spiritual privilege by relating that he'd also been given a "thorn" to keep him humble. Even Paul couldn't "pray it away," so he rested in the knowledge that God would meet his needs.

This aspect of God's grace is sometimes not one we want to hear about. We would rather that God's grace simply wipe out our suffering. But God knows that some qualities we must develop as Christians can come only through suffering. Even so, His grace is still more than enough for our needs.

Think of suffering that God has not yet removed from your life. Then write about how this suffering is helping you to become more like Christ.

_____

_____

_____

_____

_____

My Prayer for This Day:

_____

_____

_____

_____

_____

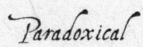

Christ Jesus came into the world to save sinners—of whom I am the worst. But for that very reason I was shown mercy so that in me, the worst of sinners, Christ Jesus might display his unlimited patience as an example for those who would believe on him and receive eternal life.

1 Timothy 1:15–16 NIV

As Paul described to Timothy his own conversion and call to the ministry, he was fully aware that God often chooses the most unlikely ways to reveal Himself. But God knows that it is through the worst of sinners, the weakest of humanity, that His grace and power are more fully evident.

Consider, as Paul did, the contrast of your life before you knew God to your life now in His grace.

My Life Before I Knew God   My Life Now in His Grace

_____   _____

_____   _____

_____   _____

_____   _____

Describe how you can use that contrast to display God's power and grace.

_____

_____

My Prayer for This Day:

_____

_____

_____

Mercy triumphs over judgment.
James 2:13 NKJV

James was exhorting his readers—once Jews under the law—to live out the mercy they had been shown in Christ, reminding them that mercy was the better way. Judgment is expected, deserved, and even right. But mercy is superior because it comes from a position of power that has every right yet chooses to forgo them. God made that very choice for us.

Name the position of power you hold right now over someone, whether it is physical, emotional, relational, or spiritual.

_____

Write a realistic scenario in which you willingly forgo your right to power in favor of showing mercy.

_____

_____

_____

_____

_____

My Prayer for This Day:

_____

_____

_____

_____

Stones of God's Mercy in My Life Day 19

Reflect back on this week's topic: the aspects of God's grace and mercy, which are . . .

* sufficient for salvation
* sufficient for suffering
* paradoxical
* triumphant over judgment

Now write your personal story of God's mercy to you this week.

_____

_____

_____

_____

_____

_____

_____

_____

_____

_____

_____

_____

_____

_____

_____

_____

A Story of God's Mercy

Mercy for Rambo

The horror and shame of Vietnam still disturbs us like an annoying fly in the summer's heat. So many healthy men and women came back from that war ravaged—unable to return to "business as usual," for business as usual seemed ridiculous after the madness they had experienced. Many others went to Vietnam as ticking time bombs, just waiting to explode. Dr. Mickey Block, a member of the Special Forces Commando, was one such person.

Mickey spent his childhood being moved from orphanages to foster homes. He had been taken out of an abusive home, his body covered in cigarette burns, and experienced the trauma of being separated from his brothers and sisters. He continued to experience abuse as he moved from home to home. His anger built, his rage grew and festered, and then he hit the killing fields of Vietnam.

Mickey's life in Vietnam consisted of drinking, killing, and frequenting whorehouses. Being sober meant facing the reality of war—seeing your best buddy killed in front of you or carrying the tiny charred body of a six-month-old baby to a medical hospital. It was a reality most wanted to escape rather than endure.

Mickey's patience with anyone talking about love in the middle of this horror quickly wore away. So he nearly went crazy when he met a man in his unit named Dave Roever. Dave was a Christian and talked incessantly about a loving God. Sometimes Mickey could hear Dave whispering prayers after the lights were out.

Mickey flaunted his habits, hoping to annoy the "preacher man." While Dave would sit on his bunk, playing his guitar and singing at night, Mickey would sit on his bunk, finishing off a case of beer.

Eight months after Dave and Mickey had been in Vietnam, a grenade exploded in the preacher man's face. Dave was transferred out of Mickey's unit, and Mickey assumed that Dave was silenced forever.

Mickey met with a similar fate one rainy evening after that. He and his company were on patrol in a free-fire zone—complete enemy territory. A young, inexperienced American crew came up behind Mickey's boat and, in the blinding rain, assumed they had come in contact with the enemy. They opened up with eight machine guns on

Mickey's boat. "It was like standing in a pitch-dark room and having hundreds of people shooting off flashbulbs in your face," Mickey said in an interview.

The bullets ripped into Mickey's body, lifting him up and throwing him to the ground. He lay there, cold and bleeding. He knew he was dying. He could hear people around him, crying and telling God they were sorry for the way they had lived. Sounds of choppers, coming to take out the wounded, echoed in the distance.

As Mickey lay in the darkness, he had a vision of Jesus hanging on the cross. Next to Jesus, another man hung, dying. Mickey could remember from Sunday school the story of the thief on the cross who deserved to go to hell. Jesus had helped that man, but Mickey felt he couldn't ask for the same help. He had lived too wretchedly. Despite his feelings, Mickey asked God to hear his life's confession. Then, everything went black.

Over the next ten years, Mickey underwent thirty-three operations. His right leg was amputated above the knee, and the skin from his chest was grafted to his left hand.

Mickey married and had two beautiful children. He had become addicted to drugs and alcohol, which almost ruined his marriage. He determined to take his own life but didn't want his children to suffer the grief of such a loss. He was alone and desperate in a living hell.

Mickey cried out to God for help but couldn't seem to reach Him. As he pondered his plight, he turned on the radio and began to listen as a Vietnam veteran talked about having lost 40 percent of his flesh to a grenade. Mickey sat up, startled.

It was the voice of the "preacher man"! And he was still talking about the love of God.

Thirteen years after they had last seen each other, Mickey and Dave were reunited. That day, Mickey discovered the mercy of God and yielded his life to Christ.

Mickey was like Jonah as he cried out to God because of his affliction. Jonah had run from the direction God wanted him to go, but he ran right into the belly of a fish. From the depths, "cast out" from God's sight, Jonah turned to God's "holy temple" and found God's mercy. He returned to God and found life and salvation in Him. Thus he was able to offer thanks to God.

I'll never understand why so many people have to experience hell before they ever taste heaven. But no matter how far you've walked away from God, when you finally cry out to Him, He can reach out and bring you back home.

Aspects of God's Grace and Mercy Day 21

For the past three weeks, you have studied fourteen aspects of God's grace and mercy, which are . . .

• for all _____

• motivated by love _____

• dimensionless _____

• abundant _____

• free _____

• enabling _____

• enduring _____

• purposeful _____

• from of old _____

• new every morning _____

• sufficient for salvation _____

• sufficient for suffering _____

• paradoxical _____

• triumphant over judgment _____

Beside each aspect, write what that means in your life.

*M*y Prayer for This Day:

_____

_____

_____

This Week's Praises, Petitions, and Intercessions

$\mathcal{R}$eserve this page for any petitions for yourself or intercessions for others that have come to your mind and heart as you journal this week. Go to God in prayer and record how and when He answers you. Praise Him for His tender, loving care.

PETITIONS

ANSWERS

_____

_____

_____

_____

_____

_____

_____

_____

INTERCESSIONS

ANSWERS

_____

_____

_____

_____

_____

_____

_____

_____

Getting to Know Our Merciful Father:
What Grace and Mercy Reveal About God

We know that our God is full of mercy. But that trait of His does not stand alone. In fact, the more you consider His gracious and merciful nature, the more you see His many other parts, which often help reveal why He could be so merciful in the first place. For example, to know God is loving helps us to know why mercy is His desire. To know that He is sympathetic is to know that God's mercy arises out of deep feeling.

None of God's traits stand alone. They all work together and play off each other perfectly, which you will see as you explore some of His traits each week. The more we understand how God's personality functions, the more we are able to direct our own fragmented personalities into greater symphony, closer to the whole image of God.

But God, who is rich in mercy, because of His great love with which He loved us . . . made us alive together with Christ.

Ephesians 2:4–5 NKJV

Paul wrote these words right after he reminded the Ephesians of their position before they were in Christ. God's love and mercy are a powerful combination. His love is immense and has compelled Him to call on His vast mercy so as not to leave His loved ones without a solution to their sin. His love wants the best for us; His mercy works to provide the solution.

Express in writing how you feel about the extent of God's love and the lengths He went to for you as His loved one.

_____

_____

_____

_____

_____

_____

_____

My Prayer for This Day:

_____

_____

_____

_____

_____

*Therefore the L*ORD *longs to be gracious to you,*

And therefore He waits on high to have compassion on you.

*For the L*ORD *is a God of justice . . .*

He will surely be gracious to you at the sound of your cry; when He hears it, He will answer you.

Isaiah 30:18–19 NASB

In the middle of Isaiah's condemnation of the sin of Israel and Judah, he refers to the merciful nature of God and His just nature. God longs and desires to give us mercy, but because of His just nature He must see repentance on our part before we can partake of it. So He waits.

*L*ist anything in your life for which you have not yet shown repentance.

_____

_____

_____

_____

_____

_____

*M*y Prayer for This Day:

_____

_____

_____

_____

_____

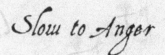

The LORD is merciful and gracious,
Slow to anger, and abounding in mercy.
Psalm 103:8 NKJV

Knowing all that the Israelites had done against God, David praised God for being slow to anger. God alone sees in black and white—He knows exactly what is wrong and right, can see motives, and has every right to be angry when anger is called for. Yet He has shown amazing restraint—He knows the power and consequences of anger and uses it judiciously. Only a merciful God would do that.

Consider the following questions and then write about what is true for you right now: What is your habit of dealing with anger? Do you restrain it for merciful and judicious purposes, or do you let it reign freely?

_____

_____

_____

_____

_____

_____

_____

My Prayer for This Day:

_____

_____

_____

_____

_____

I will sing of the mercies of the LORD forever;
With my mouth will I make known Your faithfulness to all generations.

Psalm 89:1 NKJV

This verse opens a psalm that was written in affliction. The psalmist began by praising God for His faithfulness. In his deep despair he was reminding himself of the history of God's previous faithfulness. It is just that—God's unblemished record of past faithfulness—that gives us hope that He will come to us yet again, mercifully making His presence known in our affliction.

*W*rite about God's record of faithfulness to you personally.

_____

_____

_____

_____

_____

_____

_____

_____

_____

*M*y Prayer for This Day:

_____

_____

_____

_____

For You, LORD, are good, and ready to forgive,
And abundant in mercy to all those who call upon You.
Psalm 86:5 NKJV

This prayer of David praises God for His merciful nature that is always prepared to forgive. When we ask for forgiveness with a repentant heart, God gives it without fail. And since forgiveness brings renewal to our relationship with God, it is remarkable that we don't spend more time seeking it.

*R*elate a time when your relationship with God was renewed after you sought forgiveness for neglected sin.

_____

_____

_____

_____

_____

_____

_____

_____

*M*y Prayer for This Day:

_____

_____

_____

_____

_____

Reflect back on this week's topic: the aspects of God's character, which are . . .

- loving
- just
- slow to anger
- faithful
- forgiving

Now write your personal story of God's mercy to you this week.

_____

_____

_____

_____

_____

_____

_____

_____

_____

_____

_____

_____

_____

_____

_____

_____

_____

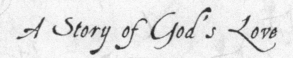

Love That Doesn't Give Up

John Shelton stood in court and listened as he was sentenced to two consecutive life terms in a mental facility for the criminally insane. As he was led away, he cursed God. "This isn't what I turned myself in for, God. You've turned on me!"

He had never known love from a person, much less from God. John was raised in an abusive home by an alcoholic mother who made her living as a prostitute. She married for the first time when she was eleven years old, and again six times after that. From the time he was six years old until he was twelve, John was sexually abused by a close female relative. When he was eight years old, he was raped by his uncle, who had just been released from prison. The abuse continued for several nights until John got the courage to tell his mother. She then attacked her brother with an iron skillet and almost killed him.

For John, the nightmare lived on outside his home. At school, the other children nicknamed him "the termite" because he was short. He felt alone and afraid.

"By the time I was a young adult," says John, "my inner rage had reached a boiling point." He felt as if the world owed him, and he set out to take revenge. He brought a .44-caliber Magnum and began a brutal spree of robbery and rape. For the first time in his life, he felt as if he were in control.

Early one August morning, John broke into a home with the intention of robbing and assaulting the woman who lived there alone. He went up to her room where she was asleep, pointed his gun at her head, and told her to do whatever he asked. Much to John's amazement, the woman opened her eyes and calmly replied, "Sir, you can do anything you want temporarily to my mind; you can do something temporarily to my body; but praise God, you can't touch my spirit!"

The woman then leapt out of bed and began to thank God for sending this needy young man to her home. John dropped his gun in surprise. The woman scooped up the gun and told him to follow her—she was going to fix him some breakfast. After they had eaten and John had gotten up to leave, she hugged him and told him that God had a master plan for his life. Motivated to change the direction of his life, John went straight from her home to the police station to turn himself in, never expecting he

would be sentenced to two life terms in prison.

The mental facility where John was sent was bleak and depressing. His anger and his feeling that he had been betrayed by God festered each day he was there.

One day a tall, well-built man with a perpetual smile came to see John Shelton. He introduced himself as John Misko, and he told Shelton that he had come to tell him of God's love. Shelton's first thought was that he was in prison because of one religious nut—he had no intentions of listening to another. But Misko wouldn't go away. For five years he visited Shelton, withstanding his constant abuse and swearing.

Nothing in John Shelton's life spoke of a God of peace and love like the lady who refused to be afraid and the man who refused to stop loving him. These two people did not get tired or give up, even when their physical bodies and personal dignity were threatened.

The apostle Paul understood threats and persecution. He chronicled his experiences and those of his companions in 2 Corinthians 4:8–9 (NKJV): "We are hard-pressed on every side, yet not crushed; we are perplexed, but not in despair; persecuted, but not forsaken; struck down, but not destroyed." Neither Paul nor his companions gave up amidst their sufferings. They rejoiced, knowing that Christ's life was being seen through their lives and that others were coming to know Christ because of their sufferings. They also held on to the hope that one day they and the ones they loved would be with Jesus forever (v. 14). And so would John Shelton.

After five years of being visited by John Misko, Shelton got down on his knees and asked Christ to set him free of the prison inside his heart. He asked the Lord to help him forgive those who had wounded him and to forgive him for wounding so many others.

Many people in our world today are filled with rage and hatred. As we hang on to the hope of everlasting life with God, we will reach beyond our barriers of safety to love others. And we will begin to see that even the most callous heart can be transformed by unrelenting love.

This Week's Praises, Petitions, and Intercessions

Reserve this page for any petitions for yourself or intercessions for others that have come to your mind and heart as you journal this week. Go to God in prayer and record how and when He answers you. Praise Him for His tender, loving care.

PETITIONS

ANSWERS

_____

_____

_____

_____

_____

_____

_____

_____

_____

_____

INTERCESSIONS

ANSWERS

_____

_____

_____

_____

_____

_____

_____

_____

_____

_____

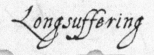

But You, O LORD, are . . .
Longsuffering and abundant in mercy and truth.
Psalm 86:15 NKJV

In one of his prayers, David, the psalmist, praised God for His longsuffering, which is one of the most direct results of mercy. Because God has so much mercy toward man, He waits until the last possible moment to execute His justice, even though it eventually must come to pass. He is the originator of the "grace period," giving us as long as He can, desiring us to come to Him. But His longsuffering toward man gives a window of mercy that will not last forever.

_R_emember a time when you made good use of God's longsuffering.

_____

_____

_____

_____

_____

_____

_____

_M_y Prayer for This Day:

_____

_____

_____

_____

_____

Wise

[God] lavished [his grace] on us with all wisdom and understanding.

Ephesians 1:8 NIV

Unlike the world, which would say that God's grace is a foolish thing, Paul made a point to praise God for His wisdom in giving us grace. One reason His grace is so powerful: It was given with eyes wide open—with total wisdom and understanding. God knew fully the ramifications of grace and yet lavished it on us.

Consider other choices God asks us to make that seem foolish to the world. List as many as you can, then go back and write about what makes those choices wise in God's sight.

CHOICES UNUSUAL WISDOM

_____ _____

_____ _____

_____ _____

_____ _____

_____ _____

_____ _____

_____ _____

My Prayer for This Day:

_____

_____

_____

_____

_____

Providing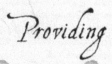
Day 10

And my God shall supply all your need according to His riches in glory by Christ Jesus.

Philippians 4:19 NKJV

Despite repeated assurances from Scripture, like this word by Paul to the Philippian Christians, we sometimes find ourselves doubting that God will provide for our needs. But worry is futile, because God has too much mercy to leave us without provision. As Paul pointed out, God has already given us Christ, and all of Christ's riches are ours as well. So our needs will be met and then some.

_D_escribe some needs that God has provided for you, despite your anxiety about them.

_____

_____

_____

_____

_____

_____

_____

_____

_____

_____

_M_y Prayer for This Day:

_____

_____

_____

_____

_____

Kind

Praise the LORD, all you Gentiles!
Laud Him, all you peoples!
For His merciful kindness is great toward us.

Psalm 117:1–2 NKJV

This brief psalm of praise extols the kindness God has shown to all people. God knows best how to show kindness, a behavior that demonstrates respect, courtesy, and compassion all at the same time. But among humans it seems a lost art, even among many Christians.

*D*escribe a situation in your life right now that calls for godly kindness from you.

_____

_____

_____

_____

_____

_____

_____

_____

_____

*M*y Prayer for This Day:

_____

_____

_____

_____

Good

> *The Lord is good to all,*
> *And His tender mercies are over all His works.*
>
> Psalm 145:9 NKJV

In this psalm of praise, David extolled the great things God had done and called Him "good." What David saw as good is that God covers everything He does with mercy.

Think of some of the works you do as God's child. Name specific ways you can imitate God's goodness and cover your work with mercy.

MY WORKS	WAYS TO IMITATE GOD'S GOODNESS
_____	_____
_____	_____
_____	_____
_____	_____
_____	_____
_____	_____
_____	_____
_____	_____

My Prayer for This Day:

_____

_____

_____

_____

_____

Reflect back on this week's topic: the aspects of God's character, which are . . .

* longsuffering
* wise
* providing
* kind
* good

*N*ow write your personal story of God's mercy to you this week.

_____

_____

_____

_____

_____

_____

_____

_____

_____

_____

_____

_____

_____

_____

_____

_____

Jesus on Skid Row

"When visitors drop by at mealtime, never ask if they've had dinner," Willie Jordan's mom used to say. "If they haven't, they might be too embarrassed to admit it. Always say, 'You'll join us for dinner, won't you?'"

Willie Jordan was raised by godly parents who had little money but a lot of love. Her mother's door was always open to her neighbors, and they knew they would find a welcome and a simple hot meal there. Willie has taken those lessons learned as a child to the streets of Los Angeles. When she was twenty-three years old, Willie married Fred Jordan. Their shared commitment to helping others drew them together with Fred Jordan Missions, which had been established in 1944 on skid row in Los Angeles.

Willie described her marriage to Fred as "magic, pure magic." They never fell out of love.

On April 4, 1988, Fred suffered a massive heart attack and was hospitalized. Willie felt she would fall apart when he died—she was certain she would want to retire from the ministry. But as she stood in her husband's hospital room, watching him take his last breath, she felt God reach out and grab hold of her. Willie became aware of the power and the presence of God as she had not been since the day she was born again when she was thirteen years old.

With the Lord's strength and joy, Willie assumed the mantle of leadership for the Fred Jordan Mission. And today the mission serves more than two thousand meals a day to poor and homeless people and sleeps two hundred and fifty people a night. It also provides job training programs, child care services, and family, marriage, and job counseling services.

In his letter to the church, James wrote of the importance of having both faith and works. "For as the body without the spirit is dead, so faith without works is dead also" (2:26). Works give life to faith the way the spirit gives life to the body. James called believers to show mercy actively to everyone—not just a select few—because God was not select in showing us mercy. How can we do this? Through our works—by giving the same honor to the poor and the wealthy, by providing food and clothing for those in need.

Willie told me of finding a woman and her five children living in a garbage dumpster behind a McDonald's restaurant. The mother was going through the trash, looking for something to give her children to eat. (More than 40 percent of the nation's homeless are women and children, who survive day to day, afraid of being raped or beaten.)

"Homeless mothers feel the same love for their children as any other mother feels for her child," Willie said. "They have the same needs, the same desire for their children to be strong, healthy, and happy. The only difference is that they don't dare to dream. I'm here to give them a dream."

I imagine that many of us are held back by fear. We are afraid to reach out to those who are different from us, as if they are an alien form of life. But with such faith as Willie's, we can see that people have the same needs, and we can show everyone the same mercy.

This Week's Praises, Petitions, and Intercessions

$\mathcal{R}$eserve this page for any petitions for yourself or intercessions for others that have come to your mind and heart as you journal this week. Go to God in prayer and record how and when He answers you. Praise Him for His tender, loving care.

PETITIONS

ANSWERS

_____

_____

_____

_____

_____

_____

_____

_____

_____

INTERCESSIONS

ANSWERS

_____

_____

_____

_____

_____

_____

_____

_____

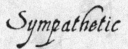

In all their distress he [the Lord] too was distressed . . .
In his love and mercy he redeemed them;
he lifted them up and carried them.

Isaiah 63:9 NIV

It is not hard to imagine God as higher than us, wiser than us. But Isaiah reminded the Israelites and us of the uniqueness of our God: When we are in distress, God sees it, feels it, and acts on it.

*R*eflect on this amazing ability of God to feel what we feel. How does that change your perspective about your trials and suffering?

_____

_____

_____

_____

_____

_____

_____

_____

*M*y Prayer for This Day:

_____

_____

_____

_____

_____

For you will go before the face of the LORD to prepare His ways,
To give knowledge of salvation to His people
By the remission of their sins,
Through the tender mercy of our God.

Luke 1:76–78 NKJV

Zechariah prophesied these words about his son, John the Baptist, who would play an integral part of revealing God's tenderness to the world. Tenderness is vulnerability and openness. This trait is what allows God His tremendous capacity for mercy.

But tenderness also indicates a willingness to be wounded. God's tender mercy, revealed ultimately through Christ, opened Him wide for being wounded, which scores of people do when they reject Him.

Describe the level of tenderness of your own spirit: Are you willing to be tender, to be open and vulnerable, expanding your capacity for godliness at the risk of being wounded?

_____

_____

_____

_____

_____

My Prayer for This Day:

_____

_____

_____

_____

_____

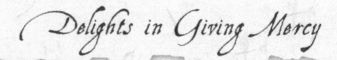

He [God] does not retain His anger forever,
Because He delights in mercy.

Micah 7:18 NKJV

Micah marveled, "Who is a God like You?" (7:18) as he contemplated that God would have mercy on the Israelites once more, despite their great sin. Showing mercy generally arises out of compassion, but God actually delights in it, desiring the opportunity. It's a good thing He does, because He has been in the position of giving mercy countless times through the ages.

*R*elate your desire to give mercy to others, answering this question: Do you delight in doing it, or do you do it grudgingly?

_____

_____

*N*ame people to whom you will extend mercy this week:

_____

_____

_____

_____

*M*y Prayer for This Day:

_____

_____

_____

_____

_____

One Who Keeps Covenant

> . . . our God,
> *The great, the mighty, and awesome God,*
> *Who keeps covenant and mercy.*
>
> Nehemiah 9:32 NKJV

After Nehemiah led the people of Israel in restoring the wall around Jerusalem, Ezra led them to restore their covenant with God. God has a perfect record of covenant-keeping, which has involved a lot of mercy-showing on His part so the people knew they were the breakers of the covenant, not God. We, however, like the Israelites, sometimes enter our covenant with Him lightly.

*W*rite about your commitment level to the covenant you have made with God.

_____

_____

_____

_____

_____

_____

_____

*M*y Prayer for This Day:

_____

_____

_____

_____

_____

Reflect back on this week's topic: the aspects of God's character, which are . . .

* sympathetic
* tender
* delights in giving mercy
* keeps His covenant

Now write your personal story of God's mercy to you this week.

_____

_____

_____

_____

_____

_____

_____

_____

_____

_____

_____

_____

_____

_____

_____

_____

_____

_____

Ceiling Fan or Mercy Stone?

*N*ot long ago I was pleased to receive another letter, which told a story of God's mercy in the life of my dear friend Pat Sands:

I still remember the time when everything in my life seemed to be going downhill. God did not even seem to be aware of my existence. I had given up one of my part-time jobs, and the other one had slacked off because of a family crisis. I knew that the second job would pick up again, but that didn't do much to relieve the stress of the moment.

The bottom line was, there just wasn't enough money to go around, and that weighed very heavily on me. And I had just been informed that I was diabetic and evidently had been for some time. The doctor told me all the damage that this "silent killer" was doing to my body; he advised me to go on a very strict nutritional plan (a sophisticated name for a diet). Ugh!

Since my last child left home about six years ago, I have lived alone; I have been divorced for more than twenty-four years. At times I am content with my status. Other times I feel very lonely. Recently I learned that one friend (who had only been divorced for two years) had a boyfriend; another friend had met a companion via the Internet. These new budding romances caused me to feel very alone and unwanted.

Is it any wonder that I felt God was ignoring me? I had prayed many times for my finances, my health problems, my desire for a companion. No answer.

Then, in the spring of 1999, I painted my living room a very soft blue and put up new curtains. When I walked into the room, I felt peaceful. I thoroughly enjoyed reclining in my comfortable blue recliner. But my home was not air-conditioned, and with summer quickly approaching I thought, *Soon I won't be able to enjoy this room because it will be so hot.*

One weekend my daughter and her husband and children drove to West Virginia for a visit. My son-in-law came into the house with a huge box and said, "God told me to get this for you."

Notice, he did not say, "We wanted to get something for you" or "Look what we bought for you." Instead he said, "God told us . . ."

In that large box was a beautiful, fifty-two-inch ceiling fan—and all the fixtures to install it.

My son-in-law had even brought all the paraphernalia necessary to mount the fan-light as a lovely swag in my ceiling, which did not have an electrical outlet.

I repeatedly thanked my daughter and son-in-law, trying to let them know how much I appreciated their thoughtfulness. "God will bless you a thousandfold," I told them.

When they left that evening, I turned on the beautiful fan, leaned back in my recliner, and stared heavenward with a sense of awe and thanksgiving.

I still don't know why God chose to give me the ceiling fan, but I believe it was His reassurance that He does see, He does care, He is concerned—and He is taking care of me and everything that concerns me.

Each time Pat sees that beautiful fan, she is reminded of the sympathetic aspect of God's character. When we are in distress, God sees it, feels it, and acts on it.

What Grace and Mercy Reveal About God

For the past three weeks, you have studied fourteen characteristics of God. He is . . .

• loving _____

• just _____

• slow to anger _____

• faithful _____

• forgiving _____

• longsuffering_____

• wise _____

• providing_____

• kind _____

• good_____

• sympathetic _____

• tender_____

• He delights in giving mercy. _____

• He keeps His covenant._____

Beside each aspect, write what that means in your life.

*M*y Prayer for This Day:

_____

_____

_____

This Week's Praises, Petitions, and Intercessions

*R*eserve this page for any petitions for yourself or intercessions for others that have come to your mind and heart as you journal this week. Go to God in prayer and record how and when He answers you. Praise Him for His tender, loving care.

PETITIONS

ANSWERS

_____

_____

_____

_____

_____

_____

_____

_____

INTERCESSIONS

ANSWERS

_____

_____

_____

_____

_____

_____

_____

_____

_____

The Blessed:

Those Who Receive Grace and Mercy

*I*t is not possible to earn God's love or mercy. He simply loves us, and His mercy is a product of His love. But God has a give-and-take relationship with His creation. While God does not cater to our whims (nor does He let us manipulate Him), He does respond with loving mercy when we give our lives to Him. So we find many references in Scripture to the kind of people to whom God loves to respond and who receive His mercy. Often behavior is the key—but a behavior that stems from a genuine heart.

Over the next three weeks, you will learn about the characteristics of the recipients of God's mercy. Try to incorporate these traits into your own walk with God, making one of your goals to be in the most open position to receive mercy.

Who Serve God with All Their Hearts

LORD God of Israel, there is no God in heaven or on earth like You, who keep Your covenant and mercy with Your servants who walk before You with all their hearts.

2 Chronicles 6:14 NKJV

In his prayer at the dedication of the temple, Solomon's words expressed what God has always wanted from us—our hearts. This is the basis for a right relationship with Him. And when God sees one of His servants who is wholehearted, nothing could please Him more. After all, what more can we give?

In which areas of your life are you serving God wholeheartedly? In which areas are you serving Him with less than your whole heart?

_____

_____

_____

_____

_____

_____

_____

_____

_____

My Prayer for This Day:

_____

_____

_____

_____

_____

He who covers his sins will not prosper,
But whoever confesses and forsakes them will have mercy.
Proverbs 28:13 NKJV

This proverb, written by Solomon, reinforces what God has established: We cannot receive mercy until we confess our sin—until we acknowledge it and repent. Confessing exhibits a humility that puts us in the position to receive mercy. Not confessing either means that we do not see our sin or we will not admit it.

Write a confession before God of sin you may be holding back from Him.

_____

_____

_____

_____

_____

_____

_____

_____

My Prayer for This Day:

_____

_____

_____

_____

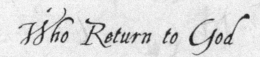

Let the wicked forsake his way,
And the unrighteous man his thoughts;
Let him return to the LORD,
And He will have mercy on him.

Isaiah 55:7 NKJV

Taken from a prophetic passage describing Jesus' invitation to the world, these words are powerfully true for us as long as we are alive. No matter how far we get from God, we can always start over with Him. But it begins with returning—going back toward Him, which requires motion on our part. God has not moved; He is standing in the same place He's always been.

Describe your position in relation to God. Have you moved away from Him or are you close by?

_____

_____

_____

_____

_____

_____

My Prayer for This Day:

_____

_____

_____

_____

_____

Therefore know that the LORD your God, He is God, the faithful God who keeps covenant and mercy for a thousand generations with those who love Him and keep His commandments.

Deuteronomy 7:9 NKJV

Moses was not afraid to talk about obedience in relation to God's covenant with people. But sometimes we are, because we fear that it will somehow discount what God has done for us. The truth is that obedience has always mattered to God—but He wants it as a response out of love for Him.

*T*hink about ways you obey God.

_____

_____

_____

*N*ow examine your motives: Do you obey out of love?

_____

_____

_____

*W*rite about how obeying out of love might change what you do or how you do it.

_____

_____

_____

*M*y Prayer for This Day:

_____

_____

_____

But the mercy of the LORD is from everlasting to everlasting
On those who fear Him.

Psalm 103:17 NKJV

In this psalm of praise, David mentioned freely the fear of God, yet fearing God has fallen out of favor with modern Christians. It comes across as negative, so we tend to shy away from it. But God talks about fearing Him in His Word, and fear is an important element of our relationship to Him.

Describe your level of fear toward God. Do you have a healthy fear, or have you lost the sense of His authority?

_____

_____

_____

_____

_____

_____

_____

_____

My Prayer for This Day:

_____

_____

_____

_____

Stones of God's Mercy in My Life

Reflect back on this week's topic: the blessed, those who receive grace and mercy. They are those who . . .

- serve God with all their hearts
- confess and forsake sin
- return to God
- love God and keep His commandments
- fear God

Now write your personal story of God's mercy to you this week.

_____

_____

_____

_____

_____

_____

_____

_____

_____

_____

_____

_____

_____

_____

Walk in Truth

When I was a little girl, I often struggled with telling the truth. I remember one day when I was about ten years old. My mom was expecting guests for dinner. She spent hours getting everything ready. Fifteen minutes before her guests were to arrive, I went upstairs to my room to see if I could find something to play with. I was bored.

The previous Christmas, an aunt had given me a glass dog filled with bubble bath, and I decided that this would be a good thing to play with now. I sat on the top stair and gave it a little push to see if it could bounce off every step on its way down. Halfway down it had gathered so much momentum that it broke, and the contents spilled all over the stairway carpet.

My mom called from the kitchen and asked what I was doing. I told her that I had dropped my piggy bank and everything was fine.

I tried to mop up the soap by rubbing it, but it foamed and foamed, until I was up to my neck in white froth. I will never forget the horrified look on my mother's face as she came into the hallway to answer the doorbell and saw me sitting on the stairs like a rabid dog, foaming at the mouth.

As I lay in bed that night, with a rather warm posterior, my mother's words rang in my ears. "I'm not punishing you because you dropped your dog; I'm punishing you because you lied to me."

What makes us afraid of telling the truth? Perhaps we fear rejection once the truth about us is known. Perhaps we wonder if people would love and accept us if they saw us as we are.

At times I have caught myself telling a story or recounting what happened at a concert or conference differently from how it was. Five hundred people may have attended a conference, but in my story eight hundred showed. Ten people may have been saved at a concert, but in my story, fifteen were saved. It's ridiculous to exaggerate what God has done. Deep down, I must feel that results impress people rather than character. But I don't think I'm alone in this.

I agreed to sing at a crusade for a lesser-known evangelist whom I had met at a conference. This man impressed me with his sincerity and his heart for evangelism, so I

was happy to participate in the event.

The evening of the crusade was a good one. About one thousand people attended, and at the end of the message, about fifty people came forward.

A few months later, this gentleman's newsletter came to me in the mail. I flipped past exciting stories of recent crusades to the article about the conference I had participated in. According to the article, about five thousand people had attended the conference, and more than a thousand responded to the gospel message. I was horrified.

As I sat in my office, full of "righteous indignation," I felt the Lord holding a mirror in front of my face, and I looked strangely like my exaggerating friend!

David's prayer in Psalm 86 has become a source of encouragement for me since this experience. "Teach me Your way, O LORD; / I will walk in Your truth" (v. 11 NKJV). David wanted to live according to God's will and according to the truth about God. He also wanted a "united heart"—a heart that stayed focused on the truth about God, a heart that was not wandering from the truth—so he could fear, or honor, God.

The truth is that God is great; He is full of power and mercy and loving care. David had recognized this truth and was praising God for it: "For You, LORD, are good, and ready to forgive . . . For You are great, and do wondrous things" (Ps. 86:5, 10 NKJV). When we trust God's greatness and mercy as David did, we are free of the need to affirm our own names and can instead fear God's name.

I keep a tight reign on myself now, and if I blow it, I publicly apologize and correct myself. God is Truth, and anything else, no matter how mild-mannered, comes from the father of all lies. I pray I will fear the Lord more than I fear my fellow man. I do not want to give the enemy a foothold in my life; I want to walk in the light. I've decided to stop exaggerating, even if it takes me sixteen million years to get there!

This Week's Praises, Petitions, and Intercessions

*R*eserve this page for any petitions for yourself or intercessions for others that have come to your mind and heart as you journal this week. Go to God in prayer and record how and when He answers you. Praise Him for His tender, loving care.

PETITIONS

ANSWERS

_____   _____
_____   _____
_____   _____
_____   _____
_____   _____
_____   _____
_____   _____
_____   _____

INTERCESSIONS

ANSWERS

_____   _____
_____   _____
_____   _____
_____   _____
_____   _____
_____   _____
_____   _____
_____   _____

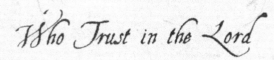
Who Trust in the Lord — Day 8

Many sorrows shall be to the wicked;
But he who trusts in the LORD, mercy shall surround him.
Psalm 32:10 NKJV

In a psalm David wrote after receiving forgiveness from God, he was certainly in a position to speak to the wisdom of trusting God—wisdom he had learned the hard way. He knew all too well the consequences of trusting in his own fallible judgment. Those who trust in God, however, are surrounded by His mercy, even when they can't see or feel it.

*N*ame ways you can show your trust in God for your situation today, even if you have no visible evidence of His mercy.

_____

_____

_____

_____

_____

_____

_____

_____

*M*y Prayer for This Day:

_____

_____

_____

_____

_____

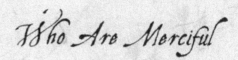

Blessed are the merciful,
For they shall obtain mercy.
Matthew 5:7 NKJV

In Jesus' Sermon on the Mount, He described His "new world order"—the kingdom of God—and how its inhabitants would behave. Showing mercy, which He mentioned here, is not a typical trait among those who are not in the kingdom.

Specify some ways that you personally, as a child of the King, can show mercy to people who are not in the kingdom (name specific people and situations).

_____

_____

_____

_____

_____

_____

_____

_____

_____

My Prayer for This Day:

_____

_____

_____

_____

_____

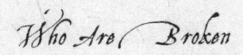
The LORD is near to those who have a broken heart,
And saves such as have a contrite spirit.

Psalm 34:18 NKJV

Out of his own deliverance experience, David described the kind of people to whom God responds: those with broken hearts. When our hearts are broken, then pride is absent, and we are willing to submit to God and open to receiving what He has for us.

*M*easure your level of brokenness by writing about your current level of pride. (Be sure to mention specific areas in your life—pride in your appearance, your home, your children.) When can this pride be good? When can it be destructive?

_____

_____

_____

_____

_____

_____

_____

_____

*M*y Prayer for This Day:

_____

_____

_____

_____

_____

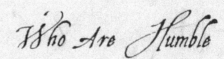

Who Are Humble

God resists the proud,
But gives grace to the humble.
James 4:6 NKJV

In this context James was talking about submission, in contrast to the selfish ways his readers had been living. Submitting—or humbling ourselves—is what God wants. It implies that we first know God's will and then choose it with a humble spirit.

*N*ame several situations in which God is waiting for you to humble yourself and submit to His will.

_____

_____

_____

_____

_____

_____

_____

_____

_____

_____

*M*y Prayer for This Day:

_____

_____

_____

_____

Who Love God's Name

Turn to me and have mercy on me,
as you always do to those who love your name.
Psalm 119:132 NIV

In the middle of instructing his readers about the importance of desiring and dwelling on God's words, the psalmist mentioned those "who love God's name." To the people of this time, God's "name" was synonymous with His character. And for those who love God's character, it is natural to seek Him in His words.

*I*llustrate how much you love God's name by revealing how much time you spend dwelling in His Word.

_____

_____

_____

_____

_____

_____

_____

_____

*M*y Prayer for This Day:

_____

_____

_____

_____

_____

Reflect back on this week's topic: the blessed, those who receive God's grace and mercy. They are those who . . .

- trust in the Lord
- are merciful
- are broken
- are humble
- love God's name

*N*ow write your personal story of God's mercy to you this week.

_____

_____

_____

_____

_____

_____

_____

_____

_____

_____

_____

_____

_____

_____

With Jesus in Paradise

*M*ost of the film people I interviewed on television were on-camera personalities. I rarely had the opportunity to talk with people who are "the brains behind the scenes," such as Bryan Hickox. Before I ever met Bryan, I was familiar with his work as a director. I had enjoyed *Troop Beverly Hills*, with Shelley Long, and was impressed by *Small Sacrifices*, which starred Farrah Fawcett.

As a Christian in Hollywood, Bryan desires to illuminate life. He looks for stories that uphold integrity and morality without forcing religious ideology. His is a strong voice for truth and humanity in a bent and dehumanizing world.

I interviewed Bryan on *Heart-to-Heart*; he was discussing a CBS after-school special called *Dead Wrong*. Usually I view movie clips before we go on the air, but that day the clips were being edited up until airtime. So I was unprepared for what I was about to see.

Dead Wrong told the story of John Evans III, who was imprisoned and sentenced to death by electrocution for killing a pawnbroker in front of his young family. It was a brutal and heartless crime.

While in prison, John came face-to-face with Jesus Christ, and he cried out to Jesus to save his soul. He was broken and he knew it. His conversion was like that of the thief on the cross who asked Jesus to show mercy on him in his last moments on earth. As Jesus was hanging on the cross, the criminal on one side of Him joined the mocking crowds: "If you are the Christ, save Yourself and us" (Luke 23:39). But the thief on the other side recognized Jesus and responded to the criminal, "Do you not even fear God, seeing you are under the same condemnation? And we indeed justly, for we receive the due reward of our deeds, but this Man has done nothing wrong" (Luke 23:40–41). This thief recognized his need and his Savior. And he received the promise of being with Jesus in paradise that very day.

John Evans's glorious conversion came in the last days before his death. Knowing that he had little time left to serve the Lord, he made a strange and courageous choice. He asked to have his last day, including his execution, filmed as a warning to others.

Tears rolled down my cheeks as I watched John Evans's mother come to say good-bye. A devout woman, she had prayed for John for many years. Now that her prayers had been answered, she was being called on to say good-bye to him. She clung to her son until the guards told her that she had to leave. "I'll be seeing you, Mom," John cried after her. Then they took John Evans III and strapped him to the electric chair.

This was the only time I was unable to finish a program. As the director and cameramen waited for me to close the show, I sat and wept. I wept for his mother. I wept for a wasted life. I wept because John never knew God's love till the last moments. Most of all, I wept with joy, knowing that the gates of the kingdom of heaven had opened that day and God had welcomed this repentant man home. That day John Evans was with Jesus in paradise.

God's mercy is limitless. We don't have to wait until a near-death experience to receive His grace. God will never turn us away when we come to Him in repentance.

This Week's Praises, Petitions, and Intercessions

*R*eserve this page for any petitions for yourself or intercessions for others that have come to your mind and heart as you journal this week. Go to God in prayer and record how and when He answers you. Praise Him for His tender, loving care.

PETITIONS

ANSWERS

_____

_____

_____

_____

_____

_____

_____

_____

_____

INTERCESSIONS

ANSWERS

_____

_____

_____

_____

_____

_____

_____

_____

For He [God] says to Moses, "I will have mercy on whomever I will have mercy, and I will have compassion on whomever I will have compassion."

Romans 9:15 NKJV

To illustrate God's sovereignty in including the Gentiles as children of the promise, Paul reminded the Jews of Jacob and Esau. God showed favor, or mercy, to Jacob over Esau while they were still in the womb—before they even had the chance to show what they were made of. It is not comfortable to accept that we cannot always explain why God seems to show mercy to one person and not another. But if we really believe He is who He says He is, then we can rest in believing that He knows best and has a purpose for what He does.

Perhaps this seems unfair to you, but Paul also wrote in Romans 9:14, "What then shall we say? Is God unjust? Not at all!" (NIV). What we see here is the spirit evidenced in the story of the prodigal son. The elder brother was offended that the father would welcome the wandering son home, but the Father's heart of compassion is not dictated by human reason or sense of justice.

*W*rite about those to whom you have trouble showing mercy.

_____

_____

_____

*M*y Prayer for This Day:

_____

_____

_____

_____

Who Approach the Throne of Grace   Day 16

Let us therefore come boldly to the throne of grace,
that we may obtain mercy and find grace to help in time of need.
Hebrews 4:16 NKJV

The writer of Hebrews made it clear that with Christ as our high priest, we can find mercy when we are in need because He understands where we are coming from. The previous verse says He can "sympathize with our weaknesses" because He was tempted in every way that we are. Because of Christ's complete understanding of our need, we can not only go to Him, but go boldly, fully expecting Him to be ready to help with sympathy and mercy.

Write what you would say as you boldly approach the throne of grace for a situation you need help with right now.

_____

_____

_____

_____

_____

_____

_____

My Prayer for This Day:

_____

_____

_____

_____

_____

Therefore, since we have been justified through faith, we have peace with God through our Lord Jesus Christ, through whom we have gained access by faith into this grace in which we now stand.

Romans 5:1–2 NIV

Paul's most noted work is the book of Romans, which has the theme of God's saving grace and our access to this grace through faith. Many people in the world have a type of faith—in mankind, in technology, in finance, in spirituality, and in all other kinds of gods and religions. But God specifies that the only kind of faith that will gain access to His grace is faith in His Son, Jesus Christ.

*E*xplain why God might specify that saving faith be solely in His Son.

_____

_____

_____

_____

_____

_____

_____

*M*y Prayer for This Day:

_____

_____

_____

_____

_____

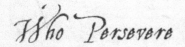
As you know, we consider blessed those who have persevered. You have heard of Job's perseverance and have seen what the Lord finally brought about. The Lord is full of compassion and mercy.

James 5:11 NIV

James encouraged believers to persevere in godly behavior as they waited for Christ's return. He referred to Job as an example of such perseverance. After Job's affliction had passed, God blessed him abundantly. Though the waiting and the trials must have seemed unbearable, Job persevered in his faith and reaped the mercy of God, who had a solution waiting for Job for just the right time.

*D*escribe how God would desire you to act in the midst of suffering when no relief is in sight. (You may want to read chapter nineteen of the Book of Job to see how this saint responded.)

_____

_____

_____

_____

_____

_____

_____

*M*y Prayer for This Day:

_____

_____

_____

_____

_____

Reflect back on this week's topic: the blessed, those who receive God's grace and mercy. They are those . . .

- whom God chooses
- who approach the throne of grace
- who have faith
- who persevere

*N*ow write your personal story of God's mercy to you this week.

_____

_____

_____

_____

_____

_____

_____

_____

_____

_____

_____

_____

_____

_____

_____

_____

_____

A Simple, Tender Message

Sometimes the women at the Women of Faith Conferences, particularly those who are married to non-Christians, say to me, "You talk about God's mercy and grace, but I have been praying for a long time and I can't see any change."

I mentioned this to my mom, and she reminded me of a man in our church who is a reserved Scotsman from the Northern Isles. The greatest pain in Jimmy's life was that his wife was not a believer. He would say, "I couldn't ask for a better wife, but it breaks my heart to think that we won't spend eternity together." He asked his friends in the church to pray for her. Year after year he asked God to reach his wife, but it was after Jimmy had died and gone to be with Christ that she gave her heart to Christ and was baptized.

It made me realize that the results are never in our hands. Our responsibility is just to be faithful, to never stop praying, to never stop living a life that would honor Christ.

One of the things I loved about Jimmy is that he never pressured his wife. God is the only one who can call you by name.

Sometimes we will not know exactly what God is doing in someone's life until we are all standing around the throne together.

For the past three weeks, you have studied fourteen characteristics of those who receive grace and mercy. They are those who . . .

+ serve God with all their hearts _____

+ confess and forsake sin _____

+ return to God _____

+ love God and keep His commandments _____

+ fear God _____

+ trust in the Lord _____

+ are merciful _____

+ are broken _____

+ are humble_____

+ love God's name _____

+ whom God chooses _____

+ approach the throne of grace _____

+ have faith _____

+ persevere _____

Look back at these fourteen characteristics. Which ones do you possess? Which ones would you like to grow in? Beside each of these characteristics, write how you might become closer to that description.

This Week's Praises, Petitions, and Intercessions

$\mathcal{R}$eserve this page for any petitions for yourself or intercessions for others that have come to your mind and heart as you journal this week. Go to God in prayer and record how and when He answers you. Praise Him for His tender, loving care.

PETITIONS

ANSWERS

_____

_____

_____

_____

_____

_____

_____

_____

_____

INTERCESSIONS

ANSWERS

_____

_____

_____

_____

_____

_____

_____

_____

_____

The Cursed:

Those Who Forsake Grace and Mercy

*A*lready in this journal we have seen the picture of God's desire to give mercy—the Scripture describes Him as literally waiting to give us mercy, waiting to see a change in our hearts and lives. But as much as the Bible talks about who will receive God's mercy, it also points out those who won't, or who by their own choices give up God's mercy and grace.

This week's study is not designed to be discouraging or to make us doubt our standing before God, which is secure if we are in Christ. But hopefully this week will make us aware of mind-sets and behaviors that are displeasing to God so that we can monitor the state of our hearts before Him.

Who Cling to Worthless Idols

Those who cling to worthless idols
forfeit the grace that could be theirs.
Jonah 2:8 NIV

As he prayed from the belly of the fish, Jonah knew that the God he served was by no means a worthless idol. After all, God had gone to quite dramatic lengths to save Jonah's life and restore him to his calling. Jonah said that those who do cling to worthless idols are barking up the wrong tree. They could have mercy with the true God; instead they cling to idols that can do nothing for them.

Describe which idols you are tempted to cling to instead of God, and how they threaten to hinder God's mercy toward you.

IDOLS

THEIR HINDRANCE

_____

_____

_____

_____

_____

_____

My Prayer for This Day:

_____

_____

_____

_____

_____

Who Show No Mercy

For judgment is without mercy to the one who has shown no mercy.
James 2:13 NKJV

James warned his readers about showing partiality to certain people, a behavior that was putting them inappropriately in the judgment seat toward others. If they wanted to play the judgment game, James reminded them, they would have to agree to the rules—if they showed no mercy, they themselves would be shown none.

*T*ake James's scenario: Imagine two people showing up in your worship assembly. One is finely dressed, obviously wealthy; the other appears homeless, dirty, dressed in rags. Examine honestly what your attitude and actions would be. (Keep in mind that some Christians can show undue prejudice against wealthy people.) Then express any need you have to balance your scale of mercy toward others.

_____

_____

_____

_____

_____

_____

_____

*M*y Prayer for This Day:

_____

_____

_____

_____

_____

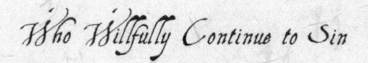

For if we sin willfully after we have received the knowledge of truth, there no longer remains a sacrifice for sins, but a certain fearful expectation of judgment.

Hebrews 10:26–27 NKJV

The writer of Hebrews issued this warning in relation to the Christian's walk of faith. There are always those who, despite the grace they have been shown, disregard it and deliberately continue to sin. Once they have disregarded Christ's sacrifice, there simply is no other sacrifice to turn to, so they forsake the only means of grace available to them.

To measure your potential for continual willful sin, describe how you regard Christ's sacrifice for your sins.

_____

_____

_____

_____

_____

_____

_____

_____

My Prayer for This Day:

_____

_____

_____

_____

_____

Who Do Not Produce Fruit

And even now the ax is laid to the root of the trees. Therefore every tree which does not bear good fruit is cut down and thrown into the fire.

Matthew 3:10 NKJV

With these words, John the Baptist indicted the Pharisees and Sadducees who had come to check up on him. John had been baptizing as a sign of repentance, but these Jewish leaders felt that being Abraham's descendants was enough to keep them in God's favor. John let them know that, as always, it is the heart that matters to God. Fruit, which is the visible, outward result of good growth, is evidence of a heart that is right. When the heart is not engaged, there is no good fruit. And where there is no fruit, John said, you can expect judgment.

Think about the condition of your heart. Then describe what kind of fruit your heart is producing.

_____

_____

_____

_____

_____

_____

My Prayer for This Day:

_____

_____

_____

_____

_____

You have become estranged from Christ, you who attempt to be justified by law;
you have fallen from grace.

Galatians 5:4 NKJV

In this passage Paul had to remind the Galatians that they were under grace and not the law, and that any attempt to be justified by the law moved them into a category other than grace. When we are not under grace, we are automatically under law and therefore subject to its consequences.

*R*eflect on times when you felt bound by legalistic laws, or when you were calling others to be bound by them. Then think about the only possible source of your justification before God.

_____

_____

_____

_____

_____

_____

_____

*M*y Prayer for This Day:

_____

_____

_____

_____

_____

Who Have No Understanding

For it is a people of no understanding;
Therefore He who made them will not have mercy on them.
Isaiah 27:11 NKJV

Through Isaiah, God told the Israelites that until they removed their idols completely, He would show only judgment toward them, and not mercy. He called them a "people of no understanding"—they were not spiritually discerning enough to know that even partial removal of idols was not enough; what remained may have seemed harmless to them but still profoundly affected their relationship with God.

Think carefully about what God wants you to remove completely from your life—your idols and influences. Make a list of them and then write your plan of removal.

IDOLS AND INFLUENCES   REMOVAL

_____   _____

_____   _____

_____   _____

_____   _____

_____   _____

_____   _____

My Prayer for This Day:

_____

_____

_____

_____

_____

Reflect back on this week's topic: the cursed, those who forsake grace and mercy. They are those who . . .

* cling to worthless idols
* show no mercy
* willfully continue to sin
* do not produce fruit
* attempt to be justified by the law
* have no understanding

Do any of these descriptions apply to you? If not, do you know someone who resembles these characteristics? How could you reach him or her?

_____

_____

_____

_____

Now write your personal story of God's mercy to you this week.

_____

_____

_____

_____

_____

_____

_____

_____

_____

This Week's Praises, Petitions, and Intercessions

$\mathcal{R}$eserve this page for any petitions for yourself or intercessions for others that have come to your mind and heart as you journal this week. Go to God in prayer and record how and when He answers you. Praise Him for His tender, loving care.

PETITIONS

ANSWERS

_____

_____

_____

_____

_____

_____

_____

_____

INTERCESSIONS

ANSWERS

_____

_____

_____

_____

_____

_____

_____

_____

God's Promises:

What Grace and Mercy Provide

*I*f you were to ask the typical Christian what God's grace provides, probably the first thing to come to mind would be salvation and eternal life. But there are a host of other benefits that God provides to those who have received His grace.

Sometimes what God gives us through His mercy is quite personal. He knows us by name and knows exactly how to "customize" His grace to meet our individual needs. Yet the items included in the next two weeks can be enjoyed by all who partake in God's grace. To examine all that God has provided would take far longer than two weeks, but you can at least begin to realize the abundance of good things the Father has given us.

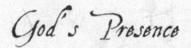

[Moses said,] "For how then will it be known that Your people and I have found grace in Your sight, except You go with us? So we shall be separate, Your people and I, from all the people who are upon the face of the earth." So the LORD said to Moses, "I will also do this thing that you have spoken; for you have found grace in My sight, and I know you by name."

Exodus 33:16–17 NKJV

When God offered His presence to the Israelites for their journey to the promised land, Moses quickly responded, realizing there was no point even in making that journey without it. He knew they faced many difficulties ahead and that without God's presence to guide, comfort, protect, and distinguish them, they might as well not even set out. Because we also have found grace in God's sight, we can expect God's presence with us for our journey.

Describe a moment you felt God's presence in your life.

_____

_____

_____

_____

_____

_____

_____

My Prayer for This Day:

_____

_____

_____

_____

*For by grace you have been saved through faith, and that not of yourselves;
it is the gift of God.*

Ephesians 2:8 NKJV

To contrast between life before and after Christ, Paul first reminded the Ephesians of the greatest human need: salvation from sin, which means we are rescued from our sin's eternal consequences. But as Paul emphasized in today's verse, our salvation must come from an outside source, because while it is a need all humans have, not one of us is able to meet it with his or her own power. God is the only One who has the ability to meet our need for salvation. And He met it by grace through Christ.

Describe the day when God, through His gracious gift of Jesus, rescued you from sin.

_____

_____

_____

_____

_____

_____

_____

My Prayer for This Day:

_____

_____

_____

_____

_____

God was reconciling the world to himself in Christ, not counting men's sins against them.

2 Corinthians 5:19 NIV

Paul saw a major goal of his ministry as sharing the word of reconciliation. The whole world needs to hear it because we all have been separated from God by our own sin. Only those in Christ will be reconciled, or brought back, to God.

*T*hink of someone who is still separated from God. Is his or her need for reconciliation urgent to you? How can you minister the word of reconciliation to that person?

_____

_____

_____

_____

_____

_____

_____

_____

_____

_____

*M*y Prayer for This Day:

_____

_____

_____

_____

_____

God made him who had no sin to be sin for us, so that in him we might become the righteousness of God.

2 Corinthians 5:21 NIV

In the context of righteousness, Paul described how it is possible for reconciliation between God and man to take place. One of the first things we forfeit the moment we first sin is righteousness. According to the law, it takes just one sin for our entire lives to be tainted with unrighteousness. Since we cannot be reconciled to God in an unrighteous, sinful state, God offered us a solution: When Christ, the perfect Lamb, died as the final sacrifice for sin, God took our sin and gave it to Christ; He took Christ's righteousness and gave it to us.

Describe what you feel as you consider the inequity of the exchange of your sin and punishment for the righteousness of Christ.

_____

_____

_____

_____

_____

_____

My Prayer for This Day:

_____

_____

_____

_____

_____

Then Peter said to them, "Repent, and let every one of you be baptized in the name of Jesus Christ for the remission of sins; and you shall receive the gift of the Holy Spirit."

Acts 2:38 NKJV

Presented with the opportunity to tell thousands of people for the first time in history about the remedy for their sin, these were the words Peter chose. Through his words the listeners found out just how merciful God is—not only had He provided a way out of their sin, but He was giving them a gift as well: His Holy Spirit. God would not go to such great lengths as to save us, then leave us on our own. He has given us divine wisdom, counsel, guidance, comfort, and power in the Holy Spirit, who comes to live in the heart of every Christian.

Describe times of the Holy Spirit's activity in your life according to some of the functions listed below.

* wisdom _____

_____

* counsel _____

_____

* guidance _____

_____

* comfort _____

_____

* power _____

_____

My Prayer for This Day:

_____

_____

Reflect back on this week's topic: God's promises, what grace and mercy provide. The Lord promises . . .

+ His presence
+ salvation
+ reconciliation
+ righteousness
+ the Holy Spirit

*N*ow write your personal story of God's mercy to you this week.

_____

_____

_____

_____

_____

_____

_____

_____

_____

_____

_____

_____

_____

_____

_____

_____

A Story of God's Mercy

Break-in, Breakout!

One weekend afternoon Beverly Courrege's infant daughter, J.J., was sleeping in her cradle near the bed where Bev and her two-year-old son, Cord, were napping. Beverly had turned the television on low volume to cartoons in case Cord woke before she did.

Cord woke his mother asking, "Mom, who is that man?" Beverly was startled to see a grown man standing at the foot of her bed, between her and the cradle! He had a finger to his lips, signaling "Hush!"

Terror rushed through her. She didn't scream because she didn't want Cord to start crying.

The man walked across the hall to the bathroom, still watching them. He came back into the bedroom and repeated the "Hush!" gesture. Then he walked down the hallway toward their kitchen and started going through the drawers. Beverly panicked. Their only exits were the kitchen and the front door, which was adjacent to the kitchen.

Hurriedly, she grabbed the phone and called her brother-in-law, who lived nearby. In a screaming whisper, she told him there was a man in her duplex and asked him to call the police.

Bev could still hear the intruder. *What can I do?* she thought. She took J.J. from her crib and brought her in the bed with Cord and her. Beverly held the baby in one arm and wrapped her other arm around Cord. Then she cried, "Lord, help me! I don't know what to do!"

Just a moment later, Beverly "noticed" their ground-floor window for the first time. All she had to do was open the window, crawl through it with the kids, go out the backyard gate, and find someone in their neighborhood at home. Minutes later they were in the safe haven of a neighbor's home.

Meanwhile, the police arrived. The intruder turned out to be the twenty-seven-year-old autistic son of a neighbor's cleaning lady. He had found her front door unlocked and wandered into their house. When the police arrived, he was still in her kitchen, looking for something to eat.

As Christians, it is comforting to know that we have access at all times to the One who rescues us. When we yield our thoughts to God, we can face any evils with the confidence that He has plans for our well-being on His mind.

Beverly had heard Jeremiah 33:3 referred to as "God's phone number." It reads, "Call to Me, and I will answer you, and show you great and mighty things, which you do not know" (NKJV). On the day of their "break-in," she was so thankful that God did not have a busy signal, call waiting, or a "please hold" recording!*

---

*Adapted from *Y2J: Yield to Jesus* by Beverly Courrege (Nashville: Thomas Nelson, Inc., 1999), 1–3. Used by permission.

This Week's Praises, Petitions, and Intercessions

Reserve this page for any petitions for yourself or intercessions for others that have come to your mind and heart as you journal this week. Go to God in prayer and record how and when He answers you. Praise Him for His tender, loving care.

PETITIONS   ANSWERS

_____   _____

_____   _____

_____   _____

_____   _____

_____   _____

_____   _____

_____   _____

_____   _____

INTERCESSIONS   ANSWERS

_____   _____

_____   _____

_____   _____

_____   _____

_____   _____

_____   _____

_____   _____

_____   _____

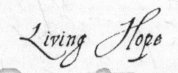 

Blessed be the God and Father of our Lord Jesus Christ, who according to His abundant mercy has begotten us again to a living hope through the resurrection of Jesus Christ from the dead.

1 Peter 1:3 NKJV

Besides salutations, these were the beginning words of Peter's epistle to persecuted Christians. He started with what they most needed—a reminder of their hope. The hope Peter reminded them of was in a Christ who lives despite His death, providing an inheritance that waits for those who believe in Him. That kind of hope produces life, renewal, and peace despite overwhelmingly bad circumstances.

*N*ame the circumstances in your life that threaten to dim your hope. Then write next to them how your hope in Christ has produced some level of renewal or peace in spite of them.

CIRCUMSTANCES   HOPE IN DEEP WATERS

_____   _____

_____   _____

_____   _____

_____   _____

_____   _____

_____   _____

*M*y Prayer for This Day:

_____

_____

_____

_____

_____

But you are a chosen people, a royal priesthood, a holy nation, a people belonging to God . . . Once you were not a people, but now you are the people of God; once you had not received mercy, but now you have received mercy.

1 Peter 2:9–10 NIV

Peter wrote his letter to Christians who were trying to "keep it together" during a time of persecution for their faith in Christ. What better way to encourage them than to reinforce their identity! The dividing line of who they were, and who we are, is God and His mercy. Before God chose us we were nothing, but once we gained access to the Father through Christ, all that changed. Suddenly we have a foundation (we were chosen by God), a function (we are a royal priesthood), and a fellowship (we are part of a holy nation).

Describe who you are personally after God's mercy, according to foundation, function, and fellowship.

FOUNDATION_____

_____

FUNCTION _____

_____

FELLOWSHIP _____

_____

My Prayer for This Day:

_____

_____

_____

_____

_____

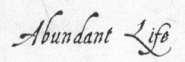

I have come that they may have life, and that they may have it more abundantly.

John 10:10 NKJV

In the context of describing Himself as the Good Shepherd, Jesus referred to why He came: that His sheep might have life more abundantly. Many people misunderstood what Jesus meant by this. But, at the very least, we can guess that the kind of life Jesus brings is in contrast to what the thief, which He mentioned in the first part of the verse, does—the one who has come "to steal, and to kill, and to destroy." The life Jesus offers is unlike the thief: Instead of stealing, it protects and restores; instead of destroying, it creates and renews.

*T*hink about the parts of your life that need restoration, renewal, or protection. Write about how Christ recently has brought life to you personally in one of these areas.

_____

_____

_____

_____

_____

_____

_____

*M*y Prayer for This Day:

_____

_____

_____

_____

_____

To this end I labor, struggling with all his [Christ's] energy, which so powerfully works in me.

Colossians 1:29 NIV

Almost as a side note in a discussion on his ministry, Paul referred to what powered all his work: Christ's energy. Apparently Paul felt Christ working in him powerfully and depicted himself as almost struggling to keep up with it. The same power to do what God has called us to do is also available for us. The gospel of John says that if we are in Christ, then Christ is in us (15:4–5). Sometimes power is a scary thing, and we are afraid to submit to where Christ's power could take us.

Describe the change that would take place in your work for God if you allowed Christ's full power to be released in you.

_____

_____

_____

_____

_____

_____

_____

_____

My Prayer for This Day:

_____

_____

_____

_____

_____

Victory Over Death

When the perishable has been clothed with the imperishable, and the mortal with immortality, then the saying that is written will come true: "Death has been swallowed up in victory."

1 Corinthians 15:54 NIV

Instructing the Corinthians on the facts surrounding the resurrection of believers, Paul built up to this crucial point: Though for most people death is the unbeatable enemy, those in Christ will have victory over it. Death holds no power over Christ's own.

*N*ame your feelings or fears about death.

_____

_____

_____

_____

*W*rite about how you feel to be on the side that wins over death.

_____

_____

_____

_____

*M*y Prayer for This Day:

_____

_____

_____

_____

_____

Stones of God's Mercy in My Life

Reflect back on this last week's topic: God's promises, what grace and mercy provide. The Lord promises . . .

- living hope
- identity
- abundant life
- power
- victory over death

*N*ow write your personal story of God's mercy to you this week.

_____

_____

_____

_____

_____

_____

_____

_____

_____

_____

_____

_____

_____

_____

_____

One Family's Living Hope

The first time I went to Christ Presbyterian Church, I noticed Brian Schraugher because he was completely bald. *Does he have cancer?* I wondered. *Is he in chemotherapy?* A month later, our pastor asked Brian and his wife to come forward during the service. Their son, Taylor, came with them. He walked up the aisle on crutches, with one trouser pinned up below his thigh. He was about ten years old and completely bald.

Brian started talking about what they had been experiencing as a family. "Our son had a tumor the size of a melon," he told the congregation. "Taylor has gone through all sorts of chemo. When his hair fell out, I said, 'I'm going to shave my hair.' Until my son gets his hair back, we will be buddies-in-baldness together.

"When the doctors decided to operate on the tumor, the surgeon warned us: 'We will try to save his leg, but there is a possibility the whole leg will have to come off.'"

Brian told the congregation about the day of the surgery. Before Taylor went under the anesthesia, Brian said he asked Taylor, "Do you understand, son, that when you wake up you might not have a leg?"

"Yes, I understand that," Taylor replied.

"Are you okay with that?" Brian asked.

"I'm okay," Taylor said.

The Schraughers waited anxiously during the many hours of the surgery. Then the doctor came out and said, "I'm sorry, we couldn't save his leg. We had to take it off."

Brian asked, "Would you let me know when I can go in and see him?"

"I'll let you know when he is conscious enough to know you are there."

Later, when Brian walked into Taylor's room, the first thing he saw was his son feeling to see if he had a leg. It broke Brian's heart. He asked Taylor if he was okay.

The boy smiled weakly and said, "Dad, there is good news in this for you."

"What do you mean?"

"Well, you should get my shoes at half price from now on!"

Taylor is an incredible kid. I watched him at Hope's birthday party. He was on the teeter-totter with the kids. He was playing soccer with Christian. He has a crutch, but he can run almost as fast as any kid. He also has a prosthetic leg, but he doesn't like to wear it. He is one of the most joyful kids I have ever known.

In the spring of 1998, I was asked to do a mini-concert on TBN during the first forty minutes of the *Praise the Lord* program. The station got a lot of positive feedback, so they asked me back again in the spring of 1999. This time I asked them if I could bring the choir from my own church, and they agreed.

At Hope's six-month birthday party, Brian came up to me and said, "You know, I wasn't looking forward to doing that TBN thing."

I asked him why, and he told me he had never been able to relate to Christian television since he didn't think it was very real. "But being there and singing with you, hearing your testimony—that's the kind of Christianity I want to be a part of."

This is why I like being part of a Christian community. One day I'm sitting in the pew, listening to Brian talk about his child, and I have tears rolling down my face, imagining what it would be like to help Christian if he had to have his leg cut off. The next moment Brian is behind me on the set of TBN, singing with me. And a month later he and I are standing side by side, sharing a burger and celebrating the life of a six-month-old baby girl.

Together we experience God's grace, and together we see how much we need each other. We are living hope for one another.

This Week's Praises, Petitions, and Intercessions

Reserve this page for any petitions for yourself or intercessions for others that have come to your mind and heart as you journal this week. Go to God in prayer and record how and when He answers you. Praise Him for His tender, loving care.

PETITIONS

ANSWERS

_____

_____

_____

_____

_____

_____

_____

_____

INTERCESSIONS

ANSWERS

_____

_____

_____

_____

_____

_____

_____

_____

Our Response to Grace and Mercy:

Taking It In

*I*ronically, one of the most difficult tasks in regard to God's grace and mercy is simply taking it in properly, if that is even possible. The immensity and scope of His grace are almost unfathomable. That can be a difficult task for our human minds. But sometimes we also struggle with its meaning and purpose. Some of us ask too much of it; others don't give it enough credit. But the gift of grace and mercy does ask for a response—it should impact our minds, our hearts, and our behavior.

The journaling for each day of this week is designed to focus on one of many components to taking in God's grace and mercy. At the end of the week, you will more fully comprehend its fullness and how your mind and heart can respond.

Rend your heart, and not your garments;
Return to the LORD your God,
For He is gracious and merciful.

Joel 2:13 NKJV

The prophet Joel pleaded with the people of Judah to repent of their sins. One argument he used was to remind them of God's great mercy—they still had time, and God was still willing. If only the world could get a real glimpse of the breadth of God's mercy in comparison to their state without Him, they would not wait but would fall to their knees in repentance.

*T*ake this space to describe what your life was like without God.

_____

_____

_____

*W*hat brought you to the point of repentance?

_____

_____

_____

*M*y Prayer for This Day:

_____

_____

_____

_____

_____

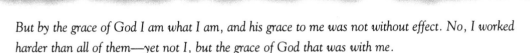

But by the grace of God I am what I am, and his grace to me was not without effect. No, I worked harder than all of them—yet not I, but the grace of God that was with me.

1 Corinthians 15:10 NIV

Maybe it was easy for Paul, with his background as a diligent Pharisee, to get caught up in the zeal of working hard for the Lord. But he never forgot the Source of his efforts. We, as Paul did, must remember that all the effort we manage to put forth is only because of God's mercy. He is the Source of all we do that is good.

*R*ecount your latest efforts for God. Then go back and identify how in reality it was God who set the stage, brought the right people, and gave the strength to make your efforts successful.

THE STAGE	THE PEOPLE	THE STRENGTH
_____	_____	_____
_____	_____	_____
_____	_____	_____
_____	_____	_____
_____	_____	_____
_____	_____	_____

*M*y Prayer for This Day:

I will be glad and rejoice in Your mercy.
Psalm 31:7 NKJV

This psalm of deliverance points out that rejoicing is a natural response to God's mercy. When we realize the deliverance God has given us from sin, our spirits naturally rise to the surface, spilling over with joy. And this happens each time we turn to God for forgiveness. Often the greater our sin has been, the deeper our response of joy.

Describe a recent encounter with God's mercy that left you overcome with rejoicing.

_____

_____

_____

_____

_____

_____

_____

_____

_____

_____

My Prayer for This Day:

_____

_____

_____

_____

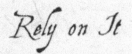

Rely on It

> *If I say, "My foot slips,"*
> *Your mercy, O LORD, will hold me up.*
> Psalm 94:18 NKJV

It is evident that the writer of this psalm understood that man's self-sufficiency is an illusion.

God continues to show us mercy despite our misplaced confidence. And His mercy is stronger than any prop we can contrive on our own. It holds us up when we run out of our own "sure" footing.

Describe a time recently when your own strength or plan gave way and instead God's mercy was there to be your support.

_____

_____

_____

_____

_____

_____

_____

_____

My Prayer for This Day:

_____

_____

_____

_____

_____

When James, Cephas, and John . . . perceived the grace that had been given to me, they gave me and Barnabas the right hand of fellowship, that we should go to the Gentiles and they to the circumcised.

Galatians 2:9 NKJV

One of the hardest things for us to do in taking in God's grace is to recognize it in others—to see and acknowledge others who have partaken of the same grace, especially if they don't follow the same tradition we've known. Even the apostle Paul's authority and fellowship were questioned until someone recognized him for who he was in God's sight.

Based on Scripture that you know, name characteristics that might help you identify those who have God's grace.

_____

_____

_____

How can you reach out to such people in grace and fellowship, and for the purpose of spreading the gospel?

_____

_____

_____

My Prayer for This Day:

_____

_____

_____

_____

_____

Stones of God's Mercy in My Life

Reflect back on this week's topic: our response to grace and mercy, taking it in. We can experience God's grace by . . .

* repenting in light of it
* knowing the source of it
* rejoicing in it
* relying on it
* perceiving it in others

Now write your personal story of God's mercy to you this week.

_____

_____

_____

_____

_____

_____

_____

_____

_____

_____

_____

_____

_____

_____

_____

_____

Love Never Fails

Sam Huddleston stood with tears rolling down his cheeks as he watched his mother walk away from her marriage and her family. A little boy, he couldn't understand what was happening. All he knew was that his momma was gone and his daddy was left to raise him, his two brothers, and three sisters by himself. A seed of bitterness took root in Sam's heart the day his mom disappeared, and the seed grew with each passing year.

In high school, Sam's friends began drinking sloe gin, and he joined in to be part of the crowd. He got so drunk the first time he tried it, he felt as if his shoes were coming out of his head. Sam's daddy, a devout Christian man, understood his son's pain and committed to help him be faithful to God. At night he would ask Sam, "Have you prayed for your momma today?" But Sam had no time for his father's God, and he got deeper and deeper in trouble.

One morning Sam came to from an all-night drinking binge in someone else's home. He turned over in bed and vaguely took in the face of the young girl asleep beside him. He heard someone knocking on a door somewhere, and he wished the person would go away. Suddenly, two police officers appeared by his bed and told him to get up and put his pants on; he was under arrest.

What did I do? Sam wondered as he sat, handcuffed in the squad car. *What could I have done?* He had no memory of the night before.

At the police station he was told that he and his cousin had burst into a liquor store, robbed it, and killed the store owner.

At seventeen, Sam Huddleston found himself in prison, sentenced to five years to life. As he lay in his cell that night, alone and afraid, he wondered if his daddy would come to see him. He felt ashamed for the disgrace he had brought on the Huddleston name.

The next day his daddy did come to see him. "Son," he said, "we're in trouble. I don't know what we're going to do, but we'll make it with God's help."

Sam soon discovered that the law of the jungle ruled in prison. It was survival of the fittest. Daily there were knife fights, rapes. The only time he felt safe was in his cell at night. And then he was haunted in his sleep by the screams of the liquor store owner, "Please don't kill me; don't stab me anymore."

One day as Sam sat alone in the prison courtyard in utter despair, he remembered something his father had once said to him: "Son, if you're ever alone and I can't get to you, call on Jesus. He'll be there."

Sam called out to the Lord, saying, "I don't believe in You, but my daddy says You're real, and he's never lied to me. If You can hear my prayer, please change my life."

That night he lay down in his cell and slept peacefully for the first night since the murder. He still had to serve his years in prison, and it was tough to live out his faith in front of his fellow inmates. But he knew that God was real. As his friends began to see a difference in him, many of them wanted to find the peace that he had found.

Sam Huddleston appeared on my show and told me his experiences. "You know, Sheila," he said, "a lot of people are skeptical of prison salvations. They think we had nothing else to turn to in prison, and that when we get out, we'll change our minds. But prison didn't change my life; Jesus did."

The day Sam was released from prison, his daddy was waiting for him. His father ran to Sam, hugged him, and took him home. That evening as they sat at the dinner table, Sam's father took a piece of paper out of a drawer. It was a note that Sam had written to him years ago, telling him that he wanted nothing to do with him or his God.

"Why did you keep it, Daddy?" Sam asked.

"Because, Son, I knew someday we would burn it together."

Huddleston never gave up on his boy. He always hoped, always trusted. A friend once told him that if Sam were his son, he would have given up on him years ago. Sam's father replied, "He's not your son—he's my son, and I'll never give up on him."

Jesus told a story of a son whose father never gave up on him. The son took his inheritance and left the village where he had grown up to have his own way in the world. According to the tradition of the culture, the father should have considered the son dead when the son left, and he should never have allowed the son to return.

But instead, Jesus said, "when he was still a great way off, his father saw him and had compassion, and ran and fell on his neck and kissed him" (Luke 15:20 NKJV).

The father had not given up on his son. He had never considered his son dead. He was waiting, watching for his son to return. He embraced his son publicly, unashamed, and even threw a party for him!

Our heavenly Father looks at us the same way. We can pack our bags, say we're tired, shake our fist at God, and walk away. But His love for us never fails. He waits for us; He watches to see when we will return. And when we do, He embraces us openly and is not ashamed of us.

The night Sam was released from prison, he and his father took a match to the note Sam had written years before, and watched its words become engulfed in flames. When it was gone, all that was left at the table was a father and his son and a love that never fails.

This Week's Praises, Petitions, and Intercessions

*R*eserve this page for any petitions for yourself or intercessions for others that have come to your mind and heart as you journal this week. Go to God in prayer and record how and when He answers you. Praise Him for His tender, loving care.

PETITIONS   ANSWERS

_____   _____
_____   _____
_____   _____
_____   _____
_____   _____
_____   _____
_____   _____
_____   _____

INTERCESSIONS   ANSWERS

_____   _____
_____   _____
_____   _____
_____   _____
_____   _____
_____   _____
_____   _____
_____   _____

Our Response to Grace and Mercy:
Living It Out

Sometimes we think of God's grace as so free that it asks nothing of us. Yet God calls us to "work out" our salvation (Phil. 2:12). This does not mean we can affect the fact of our salvation. But to make it real to us and to others, something tangible must happen after we have received this precious gift. When our behavior stems from our own attitude of mercy based on the mercy we ourselves have been shown, then tangible grace is not forced—it comes naturally. Grace will be carried out—"worked out"—in practical ways in our lives.

This week you'll reflect on several ways the Scripture says we are to make God's grace practical in our lives. After you spend time in study and contemplation, commit to incorporating these actions as you live out God's grace, knowing that each time unbelievers see God's grace in your life, they have an opportunity to respond to it.

For I say, through the grace given to me, to everyone who is among you, not to think of himself more highly than he ought to think, but to think soberly, as God has dealt to each one a measure of faith.

Romans 12:3 NKJV

After explaining the believer's position in Christ, Paul issued a caution. He knew how easy it is, once we are in the safe position that grace puts us in, to become comfortable and prideful there. The irony is that there is no place for pride in the grace-given position: it was not of our own effort. The key to humility in our state of grace is to remember our position without God's extension of mercy.

*N*ame attitudes you may have developed that are hindering you from living humbly.

_____

_____

_____

_____

_____

_____

_____

_____

*M*y Prayer for This Day:

_____

_____

_____

_____

_____

> *However, I consider my life worth nothing to me, if only I may finish the race and complete the task the Lord Jesus has given me—the task of testifying to the gospel of God's grace.*
>
> Acts 20:24 NIV

Facing "prison and hardships" (Acts 20:23), Paul still passionately clung to his task. All Christians are called to the same task as Paul: Our lives should testify to what God has done for us. In essence, it is our only task, in that it incorporates worship, evangelism, benevolence, and fellowship, all of which rise naturally from the soul that has understood what he has been given.

Consider your testimony of God's grace. How do your life and your words accurately reflect "the gospel of God's grace"?

_____

_____

_____

Describe a time when someone responded favorably to God because of your testimony.

_____

_____

_____

My Prayer for This Day:

_____

_____

_____

_____

_____

 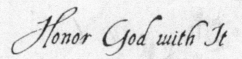

He who oppresses the poor reproaches his Maker, But he who is gracious to the needy honors Him.

Proverbs 14:31 NASB

There is really no better way to honor God than to imitate Him by showing mercy to those in need, as Solomon encouraged us to do. We ourselves had need—great need—and God was gracious to us beyond measure.

*T*hink about your attitude to those in need. How is it like God's?

_____

_____

_____

*H*ow is it unlike God's?

_____

_____

_____

*L*ist ways you can honor God by showing mercy to people you know who are in need.

_____

_____

_____

*M*y Prayer for This Day:

_____

_____

_____

_____

Let your conversation be always full of grace, seasoned with salt, that you may know how to answer everyone.

Colossians 4:6 NIV

Paul was pointing out to the Colossians that if they were in Christ, not only their inner lives but also their outer lives should be transformed. It is crucial that grace transform our speech. Paul knew of the great power of the tongue: What we say and how we speak (softly or harshly) can make or break our influence for Christ.

Describe a time when the content of your speech (what you said) was impacted by the grace you used (how you said it).

_____

_____

_____

_____

_____

_____

_____

_____

My Prayer for This Day:

_____

_____

_____

_____

_____

Paul and Barnabas . . . persuaded them to continue in the grace of God.

Acts 13:43 NKJV

When Paul and Barnabas went to Antioch in Pisidia, they knew it was important to encourage their new brothers and sisters in Christ to continue in the grace of God. They knew that in the end endurance is what counts. Sometimes we start out strong in our faith, but as years wear on us, our walk slows down to a crawl, and some of us simply stop altogether, failing to finish the race. It is important to at least keep moving—to continue, to endure, in God's grace.

How is your spiritual pace at this point in your life?

_____

_____

_____

More important, how is your endurance?

_____

_____

_____

List some strategies that will help keep you moving and continuing in God's grace.

_____

_____

My Prayer for This Day:

_____

_____

_____

Stones of God's Mercy in My Life

Reflect back on this week's topic: our response to grace and mercy—living it out. We can respond to this blessing by . . .

- living humbly because of it
- testifying to it
- honoring God with it
- speaking with it
- continuing in it

*N*ow write your personal story of God's mercy to you this week.

_____

_____

_____

_____

_____

_____

_____

_____

_____

_____

_____

_____

_____

_____

_____

_____

I'll Meet You at the Gate

*A*t 5:30 P.M. on February 3, 1998, Linda Strom was brought face-to-face with time in a way she had never experienced it. A flood of sadness rushed toward her as she hurried to the chapel at Mountain View Prison in Gatesville, Texas. She was aware of how fleeting time is and how it can simultaneously stand still.

Two days earlier Linda asked her precious friend, Karla Faye Tucker, what she would like Linda to do on February 3—the day of Karla's execution.

Her reply had been quick, soft, and yet passionate. "I'd like you to tell the women here that God is with me. He's the same in the hard times as in the good times."

At eleven the morning of the execution, Linda had started walking with several friends throughout the prison, telling the women just what Karla Faye had requested. Hearts were open and ready to hear that Jesus had paid the penalty for Karla's sins, for Linda's, and for theirs. Miracles often occur at the most unlikely times, and on that beautiful sunny Texas day, hearts were awakened to Jesus' love even as Karla went to be with Him.

In the months before the execution, Linda had reflected on how her unique friendship with Karla Faye had emerged. As Linda's husband, Dallas, once tearfully asked as he contemplated Karla's death, "How did we get here?"

Linda Strom first met Karla Faye Tucker, known to the media as the pickaxe murderer, more than a decade ago. That day she had walked from the chapel to death row at Gatesville, a little anxious about this opportunity to share Christ's love with the women there. Linda was exhausted, as she had just finished leading a weekend prison seminar. Sleeping had been a challenge the night before. Yet Linda desperately wanted God to give her words of life.

As Linda approached death row, she spotted Karla, who was smiling. She had long, curly, brown hair and dark eyes that flashed with excitement. Introducing herself, Karla gave Linda a warm hug and then started to ask questions about what had happened at the chapel seminar. Soon Linda forgot she was on death row and instead felt she was visiting an interested friend. During that time Karla told Linda how they had changed the name of death row to life row because four women were there, and each had come to know the life talked about in John—abundant life.

After several hours of meaningful conversation, Linda had to leave. Karla and she prayed and hugged one another, and Linda knew she'd be back.

Over the next ten years Linda would have many heart-to-heart visits with her friend Karla. They had the same passion for hurting women, and that created a bond between them. Karla's childhood had been painful, as had Linda's. They grew in their friendship, and they honestly confronted issues that surface when a person comes face-to-face with truth. They talked vulnerably about anger and lack of forgiveness. As Linda's life was being pruned, so was Karla's.

In November 1997, Warden Pamela Baggett called Linda to tell her about Karla's date with death, since Karla had listed Linda as her spiritual adviser. In reality Linda was to learn much about joy and surrender through Karla. They cried and shared hopes and dreams. But Christ was always their focus.

On one of Linda's last visits, Karla had joy in her face but tears in her eyes. She said, "Linda, I'll be waiting for you by the gate. See you when you get there."

The last time Dallas and Linda saw Karla was on February 1. They shared communion with her. Then they slowly and peacefully read Psalm 23 and sang "Thou Art Worthy," the song Karla requested. Although bars separated them, they still were able to interlock their fingers as they sang. Their fingers ached from the metal mesh, but it was such a gift—that gift of touch.

Then a guard reluctantly walked toward them. With compassion, she quietly told them their time was up. Karla Faye and Linda placed their faces to the bars, touched cheeks, kissed each other, and said, "I love you." Slowly Karla and Linda walked their separate ways, knowing the next time they would meet would be at heaven's gate.

During those last weeks of her life, Karla had a bride's radiance. Each morning as Linda had walked and prayed before she went to the prison, she had known she was to release Karla to her Bridegroom—but it was difficult.

On Tuesday morning, February 3, before she honored Karla's request to go to the people in prison, Linda read this passage from Revelation 19:1, 7–9:

Hallelujah!
Salvation and glory and power belong to our God . . .
Let us rejoice and be glad
and give him glory!
For the wedding of the Lamb has come
and his bride has made herself ready.
Fine linen, bright and clean
was given her to wear . . .
Blessed are those who are invited to the wedding supper of the Lamb! (vv. 1, 7–9 NIV)

In a sense, Linda had been part of the bridal party.

The hour of the execution was set for 6:00 P.M. A number of women were singing with Linda at the service in the chapel at Gatesville. Karla loved to sing. But that evening she was two hundred miles away in Huntsville, where the execution was to take place. Was she singing with them?

At 6:47 P.M., the telephone rang in the chaplain's office. The worshipers in the chapel were singing the "Battle Hymn of the Republic." As the chaplain at Gatesville announced Karla's home-going, Linda felt such relief. All she could say was, "Thank You, Father. My friend Karla, the beautiful bride, is safely home."

Later Linda learned that after Karla had been strapped onto the gurney and said her final words of love, thanks, and a brief appeal for forgiveness, she had concluded with, "I'm going to be face-to-face with Jesus now." And then she sang, probably just at the time the worshipers were singing in the chapel at Gatesville.

Two months later Linda revisited life row. A poster hanging on the wall was of Karla Faye—laughing. There were wonderful memories. That day, as she walked back to the chapel, Linda Strom lifted her eyes toward heaven and said, "I'll meet you at the gate, Karla."*

---

*Excerpted from *Just Between Friends* by Terry Meeuwsen (Nashville: Thomas Nelson, Inc., 1999), 25–30. Used by permission.

Linda Strom's book, *Set Free*, which tells the entire story of her journey with Karla Faye Tucker, will be published by Harold Shaw Publishing in Spring 2000.

This Week's Praises, Petitions, and Intercessions

Reserve this page for any petitions for yourself or intercessions for others that have come to your mind and heart as you journal this week. Go to God in prayer and record how and when He answers you. Praise Him for His tender, loving care.

PETITIONS

ANSWERS

_____

_____

_____

_____

_____

_____

_____

_____

_____

_____

_____

_____

_____

_____

_____

_____

_____

_____

INTERCESSIONS

ANSWERS

_____

_____

_____

_____

_____

_____

_____

_____

_____

_____

_____

_____

_____

_____

_____

_____

_____

_____

Moments of Mercy:
Old Testament

If there was ever any question that God's grace and mercy were reserved for the New Testament, let this week's merciful moments settle the issue. As we know by now, mercy is part of God's divine character and has been the only means for God's continued relationship with man.

This week looks not only at God's mercy to man, but also at man's mercy toward other human beings—man acting in the image in which he was created. Understanding God's mercies to man is humbling; it produces gratitude and helps us keep our pride in check. Witnessing man's mercy to man is inspiring and encouraging, giving us hope that we can do better at it ourselves. You might want to read the entire portion of each day's Scripture excerpt to fully appreciate God's mercy to us and our mercy to each other.

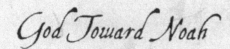
God Toward Noah

So the LORD said, "I will destroy man whom I have created from the face of the earth, both man and beast, creeping thing and birds of the air, for I am sorry that I have made them." But Noah found grace in the eyes of the LORD . . . Then the LORD said to Noah, "Come into the ark, you and all your household, because I have seen that you are righteous before Me in this generation . . . So [the Lord] destroyed all living things . . . Only Noah and those who were with him in the ark remained alive.

Genesis 6:7–8, 7:1, 23 NKJV

God had had it with the sinful world. But one righteous man caught His eye, and for that one man God was willing to spend years preparing him to be rescued—to show His mercy to one righteous man while He destroyed the rest of the world. One thing we can learn from this story is that God responds dramatically when He sees a heart trying to live right.

*W*rite about what God would see if He were looking down on the earth at you—would your heart stand out to Him?

_____

_____

_____

_____

_____

_____

*M*y Prayer for Today:

_____

_____

_____

_____

_____

[God] said to him, "Abraham! . . . Take now . . . your only son Isaac, whom you love, and go to the land of Moriah, and offer him there as a burnt offering" . . . Then [Abraham and Isaac] came to the place of which God had told him. And Abraham built an altar there . . . and he bound Isaac his son and laid him on the altar . . . And Abraham stretched out his hand and took the knife to slay his son. But the Angel of the LORD called to him from heaven and said, "Abraham, Abraham! . . . Do not lay your hand on the lad, or do anything to him; for now I know that you fear God, since you have not withheld your son, your only son, from Me." Then Abraham lifted his eyes and looked, and there behind him was a ram . . . [He] offered it up for a burnt offering instead of his son.

Genesis 22:1–2, 9–13 NKJV

God asked Abraham to sacrifice his son; Abraham could not possibly have understood, but he trusted God and obeyed. God saw Abraham's heart in complete obedience, and instead of requiring him to go through with the sacrifice, God in His mercy showed up at the critical moment and had the solution waiting in the wings.

Think of a specific situation in your life that is waiting on your obedience. Describe what your next step would be if you were fully trusting in God's timing of God's mercy and provision.

_____

_____

_____

_____

My Prayer for Today:

_____

_____

_____

_____

Then the messengers returned to Jacob, saying, "We came to your brother Esau, and he also is coming to meet you, and four hundred men are with him." So Jacob was greatly afraid and distressed . . . But Esau ran to meet him, and embraced him, and fell on his neck and kissed him, and they wept.

Genesis 32:6–7; 33:4 NKJV

The last time Jacob and Esau had seen each other, Jacob had just stolen Esau's blessing, and Esau had vowed to kill him. So when, years later, Jacob had to pass through Esau's territory, he was understandably afraid. And when he heard that Esau was on his way to meet him, he knew it must be all over.

We don't know what happened to Esau during that time, but something must have worked on his heart, because in a very emotional scene, Esau not only did not kill Jacob, but he embraced him with tears and kisses.

Choosing to show mercy and not judgment or revenge is powerful and healing for all involved. Think of a person who deserves your wrath because of what he or she has done. Write a scenario in which you instead show him or her mercy.

_____

_____

_____

Describe how it might affect you and the other person.

_____

_____

_____

My Prayer for Today:

_____

_____

And Joseph said to his brothers, "Please come near to me." So they came near. Then he said: "I am Joseph your brother, whom you sold into Egypt. But now, do not therefore be grieved or angry with yourselves because you sold me here; for God sent me before you to preserve life . . . I will provide for you, lest you and your household . . . come to poverty; for there are still five years of famine . . . Bring your father and your households . . . I will give you the best of the land of Egypt, and you will eat the fat of the land" . . . "You meant evil against me; but God meant it for good, in order to . . . save many people alive."

Genesis 45:4–5, 11, 18; 50:20 NKJV

Another story of betrayal and estrangement—something that happens frequently in families. After enduring years of slavery, false accusations, and wrongful imprisonment—all at the hand of his brothers—Joseph was in a position to be bitter and angry. And because he was now the Egyptian Pharaoh's right-hand man, he was in a position of power to avenge himself when his brothers came to Egypt to find relief from the famine in the land. Yet as this passage shows, not only did Joseph provide the necessities, he gave them the best Egypt had to offer.

How was Joseph able to keep his heart tender and even have the desire to forgive his brothers and restore their relationship? He could see and rest in God's greater purpose. Perhaps the key to having a merciful heart is to be closely in touch with what God is doing through your circumstances and despite them.

*N*ame a situation that tempts you toward bitterness. Then write a possible way it could be used for God's greater purpose.

_____

_____

*M*y Prayer for Today:

_____

_____

_____

_____

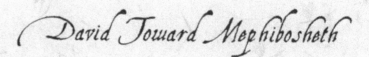

Now David said, "Is there still anyone who is left of the house of Saul, that I may show him kindness for Jonathan's sake?" . . . And Ziba said to the king, "There is still a son of Jonathan who is lame in his feet" . . . Now when Mephibosheth the son of Jonathan, the son of Saul, had come to David, he fell on his face and prostrated himself . . . So David said to him, "Do not fear, for I will surely show you kindness for Jonathan your father's sake, and will restore to you all the land of Saul your grandfather; and you shall eat bread at my table continually" . . . So Mephibosheth dwelt in Jerusalem, for he ate continually at the king's table. And he was lame in both his feet.

2 Samuel 9:1, 3, 6–7, 13 NKJV

Jonathan's death had been a severe blow to his friend King David. So even years later David wanted to do something out of respect for his dear and loyal friend. Jonathan's son was crippled and was likely considered of little use to his society. Nonetheless, David took him in and restored to him what a descendant of the king should have. David showed him mercy by taking him out of what must have been a meager life and feeding him "at the king's table." We do not know of any previous relationship between David and Mephibosheth. But it was solely the love and respect David had toward Jonathan that prompted his mercy and kindness.

*N*ame a situation in which the respect you have for one person would prompt you to go out of your way to show mercy to another.

_____

_____

_____

*M*y Prayer for Today:

_____

_____

_____

_____

Stones of God's Mercy in My Life   Day 6

Reflect back on this week's topic: moments of mercy in the Old Testament. Think of God's mercy when he . . .

- told Noah to prepare the ark
- sent the ram as the burnt offering

And then think of these instances of our mercy toward each other . . .

- Esau toward Jacob
- Joseph toward his brothers
- David toward Mephibosheth

Now write your personal story of God's mercy to you this week.

_____

_____

_____

_____

_____

_____

_____

_____

_____

_____

_____

_____

David Toward Saul

Then Saul took three thousand chosen men . . . and went to seek David . . . So he came . . . to a cave; and Saul went in to attend to his needs. (David and his men were staying in the recesses of the cave.)

Then the men of David said to him, "This is the day of which the LORD said to you, 'Behold, I will deliver your enemy into your hand, that you may do to him as it seems good to you.'" And David arose and secretly cut off a corner of Saul's robe.

Now it happened afterward that David's heart troubled him because he had cut Saul's robe . . .

And David said to Saul . . . "This day your eyes have seen that the LORD delivered you today into my hand in the cave, and someone urged me to kill you. But my eye spared you, and I said, 'I will not stretch out my hand against my lord, for he is the LORD's anointed'" . . .

And Saul lifted up his voice and wept. Then he said to David: "You are more righteous than I; for you have rewarded me with good, whereas I have rewarded you with evil. And you have shown this day how you have dealt well with me; for when the LORD delivered me into your hand, you did not kill me."

1 Samuel 24:2–5, 9–10, 16–18 NKJV

This Week's Praises, Petitions, and Intercessions

Reserve this page for any petitions for yourself or intercessions for others that have come to your mind and heart as you journal this week. Go to God in prayer and record how and when He answers you. Praise Him for His tender, loving care.

PETITIONS

ANSWERS

_____

_____

_____

_____

_____

_____

_____

_____

INTERCESSIONS

ANSWERS

_____

_____

_____

_____

_____

_____

_____

_____

Moments of Mercy:
New Testament

The New Testament has always been synonymous with grace. It is indeed the record of when God made His grace known to the world through Christ. Jesus was God in the flesh, sent to illustrate God's mercy through instruction, healing, and sacrifice. So, appropriately, most of the merciful moments this week belong to Him.

But the New Testament is full of people, including Jesus' apostles, who took their cue from the Master of mercy and began to imitate Him, multiplying the mercy they had been shown. God designed His mercy to work that way. Savor this week of observing God in action as He started it all by showing mercy as the Son of Man.

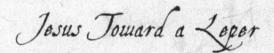

Day 1

Jesus Toward a Leper

And behold, a leper came and worshiped [Jesus], saying, "LORD, if You are willing, You can make me clean." Then Jesus put out His hand and touched him, saying, "I am willing; be cleansed." Immediately his leprosy was cleansed.

Matthew 8:2–3 NKJV

In this encounter Jesus showed right away that His mercy is truly for everyone. As most people are aware, lepers were shunned and outcast from society because of their incurable, wasting disease. They were considered unclean and untouchable. This leper believed that Jesus had the power to heal him, but wondered whether Jesus would be willing to use it on such an undesirable person as himself. Jesus responded simply by touching him and saying, "I am willing."

*N*ame types of people our society regards as undesirable, untouchable, even "unclean."

_____

_____

*W*rite about your willingness to show "touchable" mercy to these people as Jesus would have.

_____

_____

_____

*M*y Prayer for This Day:

_____

_____

_____

_____

Then the scribes and Pharisees brought to [Jesus] a woman caught in adultery. And when they had set her in the midst, they said to Him, "Teacher, this woman was caught in adultery, in the very act. Now Moses, in the law, commanded us that such should be stoned. But what do You say?" . . . [Jesus] raised Himself up and said to them, "He who is without sin among you, let him throw a stone at her first" . . . When Jesus had raised Himself up and saw no one but the woman, He said to her, "Woman, where are those accusers of yours? Has no one condemned you?" She said, "No one, Lord." And Jesus said to her, "Neither do I condemn you; go and sin no more."

John 8:3–5, 7, 10–11 NKJV

This passage of Scripture has proved to be universally touching because it so vividly depicts the tender mercy of our Lord. It was an awkward and painful situation. The punishment dictated by the woman's sin was bad enough without the added pain of this kind of humiliation. The cruelty of the Jewish leaders stood in harsh relief to Jesus' mercy, which freed the accused and convicted the accusers. By all rights the woman should have been stoned; after all, she had broken the law. But Jesus had divine authority to give her mercy, and in the process He taught some unmerciful men a crucial lesson.

*E*xplain how being aware of your own sin contributes to your attitude toward the sins of others.

_____

_____

_____

*M*y Prayer for This Day:

_____

_____

_____

_____

_____

And while [Jesus] was still speaking . . . Judas, one of the twelve, went before them and drew near to Jesus to kiss Him. But Jesus said to him, "Judas, are you betraying the Son of Man with a kiss?" When those around Him saw what was going to happen, they said to Him, "Lord, shall we strike with the sword?" And one of them struck the servant of the high priest and cut off his right ear. But Jesus answered and said, "Permit even this." And He touched his ear and healed him.

Luke 22:47–51 NKJV

The disciples must have been half in shock, half in anger as they realized that Judas was leading Jesus' killers to Him. Maybe cutting off the enemy's ear was uncalled for, but understandable considering the circumstances; compared to what Jesus would endure soon, a cut-off ear was nothing.

Imagine the effect Jesus' action must have had on the servant; his life must have been profoundly changed. He was the enemy, yet he was touched, healed, and shown mercy by the One he was out to get.

Think of the people who seem to be out to get you, hinder your career, interfere with your happiness, or worse. Name specific ways you can show them unsolicited, unexpected mercy.

_____

_____

_____

_____

My Prayer for This Day:

_____

_____

_____

_____

_____

Jesus Toward Saul

Saul [was] still breathing threats and murder against the disciples of the Lord . . . As he journeyed he came near Damascus, and suddenly a light shone around him from heaven. Then he fell to the ground, and heard a voice saying to him, "Saul, Saul, why are you persecuting Me? . . . I am Jesus, whom you are persecuting" . . . The Lord said to [Ananias], "Arise and go to the street called Straight, and inquire . . . for one called Saul of Tarsus" . . . Then Ananias answered, "Lord, I have heard . . . how much harm he has done to Your saints in Jerusalem". . . But the Lord said to him, "Go, for he is a chosen vessel of Mine to bear My name before Gentiles, kings, and the children of Israel."

Acts 9:1, 3–5, 11, 13, 15 NKJV

There was probably no greater opponent to Christianity than Saul of Tarsus. But this was nothing Jesus couldn't handle. Jesus went straight to His fierce opponent and forever changed the direction of his energies. This is the kind of change that God's mercy can effect. Where Saul was once a major force of destruction to Christianity, now he is considered by many to be the most influential of all of Christ's apostles. Jesus took someone who was tearing down the kingdom and put him in charge of its biggest building project— the evangelizing of the Gentiles.

*C*ompose a letter to Jesus in response to His tender mercy toward you.

_____

_____

_____

_____

*M*y Prayer for This Day:

_____

_____

_____

_____

[The magistrates] threw [Paul and Silas] into prison, commanding the jailer to keep them securely . . . Suddenly there was a great earthquake, so that . . . immediately all the doors were opened and everyone's chains were loosed. And the keeper of the prison, awaking from sleep and seeing the prison doors open, supposing the prisoners had fled, drew his sword and was about to kill himself. But Paul called with a loud voice, saying, "Do yourself no harm, for we are all here" . . . Then [Paul and Silas] spoke the word of the Lord to him and to all who were in his house. And he took them the same hour of the night and washed their stripes.

Acts 16:23, 26–28, 32–33 NKJV

This really is a story of mercy multiplied three times. First, God loosed the chains of Paul and Silas, who were prisoners in Philippi. Then, instead of running off with their new-found freedom, Paul and Silas—true to their calling—shared God's grace with a suicidal jailer who needed freedom from the chains of sin. In this moment of mercy, they gave him not only his life back, but eternal life as well. And in return, the jailer's first response to their word of grace was to show them grace by taking them late at night to care for their prison wounds.

This is a clear example of how God designed His mercy to carry on.

Describe an example from your life when mercy led to more mercy.

_____

_____

_____

_____

My Prayer for This Day:

_____

_____

_____

_____

Reflect back on this week's topic: moments of mercy in the New Testament. Think of Jesus' mercy toward . . .

- the leper
- the woman caught in adultery
- the servant of the high priest
- Saul
. . . and the Philippian jailer's mercy toward Paul and Silas.

Now write your personal story of God's mercy to you this week.

_____

_____

_____

_____

_____

_____

_____

_____

_____

_____

_____

_____

_____

_____

_____

_____

The Father Toward the Prodigal Son

When [the prodigal son] came to himself, he said, "How many of my father's hired servants have bread enough and to spare, and I perish with hunger! I will arise and go to my father, and will say to him, 'Father, I have sinned against heaven and before you, and I am no longer worthy to be called your son. Make me like one of your hired servants.'"

And he arose and came to his father.

But when he was still a great way off, his father saw him and had compassion, and ran and fell on his neck and kissed him.

Luke 15:17–20 NKJV

This Week's Praises, Petitions, and Intercessions

$\mathcal{R}$eserve this page for any petitions for yourself or intercessions for others that have come to your mind and heart as you journal this week. Go to God in prayer and record how and when He answers you. Praise Him for His tender, loving care.

PETITIONS

ANSWERS

_____

_____

_____

_____

_____

_____

_____

_____

INTERCESSIONS

ANSWERS

_____

_____

_____

_____

_____

_____

_____

_____

Love Stones:

God's Reminders of His Grace and Mercy

Throughout history God's grace and mercy have left their mark. It has taken many forms: Whether it be relief from judgment or provision for need, God has consistently shown mercy to His people. But because we humans tend to have a short memory, God occasionally has established symbols, rituals, or physical reminders to communicate, illustrate, or commemorate His great mercy toward His people. Some of them are universally known; some are unfamiliar. But all have served the same purpose in their time. So spend the week revisiting these reminders, and incorporate as many of them into your life as you can to always keep before you God's great mercy. Again, you might want to read the complete Scripture passages from the Bible.

"For I will pass through the land of Egypt on that night, and will strike all the firstborn in the land of Egypt, both man and beast; and against all the gods of Egypt I will execute judgment: I am the LORD. *Now the blood shall be a sign for you on the houses where you are. And when I see the blood, I will pass over you; and the plague shall not be on you to destroy you when I strike the land of Egypt. So this day shall be to you a memorial."*

Exodus 12: 12–14 NKJV*

The Passover is still an integral part of the Jewish religion, and with good reason. The Passover is celebrated as a memorial feast commemorating God's deliverance of the Israelites from slavery in Egypt. The meaning of this event is not lost on Christians; it foreshadowed when God "passes over" those of us who are covered by the blood of Jesus, the Lamb, and delivers us from death, judgment, and slavery to sin. In the Passover God has left a vivid and powerful reminder of His provision and mercy.

$\mathcal{D}$escribe specifically what God in His mercy has delivered you from.

_____

_____

_____

_____

_____

$\mathcal{M}$y Prayer for This Day:

_____

_____

_____

_____

_____

*For the entire incident, read Exodus 11 and 12.

[The Lord said to Moses,] "You shall make a mercy seat of pure gold . . . You shall put the mercy seat on top of the ark [of the covenant], and in the ark you shall put the Testimony that I will give you. And there I will meet with you, and I will speak with you from above the mercy seat, from between the two cherubim which are on the ark of the Testimony, about everything which I will give you in commandment to the children of Israel.

"Tell Aaron your brother not to come at just any time into the Holy Place inside the veil, before the mercy seat which is on the ark, lest he die; for I will appear in the cloud above the mercy seat . . . Then [Aaron] shall kill the goat of the sin offering, which is for the people . . . and sprinkle it on the mercy seat and before the mercy seat. So shall he make atonement for the Holy Place . . . for all their sins."

Exodus 25:17, 21–22; Leviticus 16:2, 15–16 NKJV

The mercy seat signified the first official meeting place for God with man. From this spot over the ark of the covenant, God gave His instruction to the Israelites—it was where God's presence came. It was also the place of atonement, where the high priest would sprinkle blood from the yearly animal sacrifice. The theory was that God would look down and see the blood, which would be sufficient to temporarily "cover" the sins of the people from the eyes of God.

Later, Christ became the final mercy seat of God. At the Cross is where you find the permanent blood sacrifice for atonement. All sinners need to do is to go to the Cross and receive the atonement and mercy that are freely and permanently given there.

*N*ame some of your own sins that have been covered by Christ's blood.

_____

_____

_____

*M*y Prayer for This Day:

_____

_____

_____

For the message of the cross is foolishness to those who are perishing, but to us who are being saved it is the power of God.

1 Corinthians 1:18 NKJV

In warning the Corinthians to be wary of wise-sounding words, Paul made a powerful point: The cross, the symbol to the world of Christ's death for sins—God's ultimate expression of grace—is foolish to those who try to make sense of it with worldly wisdom. Only those with spiritual eyes can see its true wisdom and beauty, and those are the very ones who live by its power. For so many today, a cross is nothing more than a trendy bauble or an opportunity to scoff. But for Christians it is a humbling yet powerful reminder of God's "foolish" mercy toward us.

*E*xpress the feelings and thoughts you have when you see a cross.

_____

_____

_____

_____

_____

_____

_____

*M*y Prayer for This Day:

_____

_____

_____

_____

_____

For I received from the Lord that which I also delivered to you: that the Lord Jesus on the same night in which He was betrayed took bread; and when He had given thanks, He broke it and said, "Take, eat; this is My body which is broken for you; do this in remembrance of Me." In the same manner He also took the cup after supper, saying, "This cup is the new covenant in My blood. This do, as often as you drink it, in remembrance of Me." For as often as you eat this bread and drink this cup, you proclaim the Lord's death till He comes.

1 Corinthians 11:23–26 NKJV

Jesus Himself instituted this symbol and memorial. It's hard to believe that we would need to be reminded of such an event as the death of our Lord for our sins. But we do. The bread and the wine symbolize His body and blood, the parts broken for our sakes. Each time we participate in this memorial, we have the opportunity to proclaim what Jesus has done. Not only does it remind us, but it also reminds the world. This memorial can keep us in touch with not only our Messiah but also our mission. We have a duty to proclaim Christ's death—His sacrifice for sins.

Describe why Jesus asked us to proclaim His death in this way until He comes again.

_____

_____

_____

_____

My Prayer for This Day:

_____

_____

_____

_____

_____

 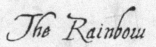

[God said,] "I have set my rainbow in the clouds, and it will be the sign of the covenant between me and the earth. Whenever I bring clouds over the earth and the rainbow appears in the clouds, I will remember my covenant between me and you and all living creatures of every kind. Never again will the waters become a flood to destroy all life."

Genesis 9:13–15 NIV

Ever since God made this covenant with Noah after the flood, people everywhere still pause to view this beautiful reminder from God that He will keep His merciful promise. The rainbow is a tangible sign that God is still with us and loves us and is protecting us, solely because of His mercy, from what we might have otherwise deserved.

Describe your thoughts and feelings when you see a rainbow in the heavens.

_____

_____

_____

_____

_____

_____

_____

My Prayer for This Day:

_____

_____

_____

_____

_____

Stones of God's Mercy in My Life

Reflect back on this week's topic: reminders of God's grace and mercy, which are . . .

- Passover
- the mercy seat
- the cross
- the Lord's Supper
- the rainbow

Now write your personal story of God's mercy to you this week.

_____

_____

_____

_____

_____

_____

_____

_____

_____

_____

_____

_____

_____

_____

_____

_____

_____

A Story of God's Mercy

Did You Say Brain Tumor?

At 6:00 A.M. one January morning in 1981, Beverly Courrege's husband left for a sales convention in Atlanta, Georgia. Bev was walking down the hallway of their home when her vision blurred, her tongue felt thick, and her hands and feet went numb, causing her to stagger shakily back to bed. She sank onto the mattress in a state of semiconsciousness.

At some point she realized she might not be able to get up. (Her children had spent the night next door with their friends, so she was alone.) By mid-morning Beverly called her sister-in-law to ask her to take her to the emergency room. Her doctor and an elder from her church met her there. By noon Beverly's brain waves and heartbeat were being monitored, and she was scheduled for more extensive testing throughout the day. Her preliminary diagnosis was grim: Her symptoms indicated that at best, she could end up paralyzed, and at worst, she could die within forty-eight hours.

Bev's sister-in-law and the church elder remained by her side, constantly comforting her and praying for her. They reached her husband, Boo, in Atlanta, and by 10:00 P.M. he was at her side to "join the watch."

The next morning, another test revealed that Beverly had a brain tumor. The doctors told her husband about the tumor that afternoon and said it would be the next day before they could tell whether the tumor was active (malignant) or benign. Bev's husband and friends decided to spare her the anguish of this new development. While she slept peacefully, unaware of this new crisis, members of her church and many other intercessors were praying on her behalf.

The second test revealed that her tumor was inactive; it was "calcified." Forty-eight hours after Beverly was admitted to the hospital with a life-threatening diagnosis, her symptoms were diminishing, some even having disappeared completely.

Her third morning in the hospital, a friend brought a hospital tray of food to her. Scripture verses were taped to each corner of the tray. Bev later learned that the tray belonged to another dear sister in the Lord who went home to be with Him after her illness with a brain tumor.

Ironically, the friend who had brought the food tray went home to be with the Lord fifteen years later. Her illness? Also a brain tumor. She had moved away, but they talked on the phone during her final months. Bev wondered silently about the "God-extraordinary" connection between the three of them. *Why them and not me?* She does not know why she was spared.

In John 9:3, Jesus told His disciples that a man had been born blind "that the works of God should be revealed in him" (NKJV). Then Christ healed the man, an example of the Lord's work in his life. Perhaps Beverly's benign tumor was a gift for the intercessors who prayed for her, because their lives were certainly yielded to the Lord. This was one instance where God's saints shared in a rich blessing.

Today, almost twenty years later, Bev's tumor is still there and is still benign. Perhaps the Lord wanted Bev to be constantly reminded of His glory working in her, reminding her to live a yielded life to the One who spared it.*

---

*Adapted from Y2J: *Yield to Jesus* by Beverly Courrege (Nashville: Thomas Nelson, Inc., 1999), 11–13. Used by permission.

This Week's Praises, Petitions, and Intercessions

$\mathcal{R}$eserve this page for any petitions for yourself or intercessions for others that have come to your mind and heart as you journal this week. Go to God in prayer and record how and when He answers you. Praise Him for His tender, loving care.

PETITIONS

ANSWERS

_____   _____

_____   _____

_____   _____

_____   _____

_____   _____

_____   _____

_____   _____

_____   _____

INTERCESSIONS

ANSWERS

_____   _____

_____   _____

_____   _____

_____   _____

_____   _____

_____   _____

_____   _____

_____   _____

A Final Note to the Reader

*M*y mother-in-law's dying has changed me. When you get the opportunity to sit with someone as she dies, you see reality. She isn't going to put up defenses or lie to you; there's not much point. Before she died Eleanor told me, "All the times I told you I didn't want you to hold me, I did want you to hold me. When I said I didn't like you, I loved you."

That was one of those moments when God washes our eyes so we can see people differently.

One day I was sitting in the mall, having my nails done by a young Vietnamese man who was talking to me about life. I asked what life was like in Vietnam, and he told me a little bit.

I asked if his family was religious.

"My mom and dad were into Buddhism, but it never helped me at all."

As he was talking my heart was aching for him. So I began praying for him as we were talking. Intercessory prayers. "Lord, help me to somehow be the mercy seat of Christ for this man."

All the while I was just listening, not jumping in like a "good evangelical" because I had the answer, but listening to him and praying for him. And then I began telling him of the mercy and grace I have received in my own life. About Eleanor. About the blessing of my marriage to Barry and the birth of our son, Christian.

I'm also turning grocery lines into lines of grace. When I'm waiting in line at Kroger, I look at the people around me. I used to think my role as a good evangelical was to give them a tract or say something to them.

As I mentioned before, now I think God is calling me to live with a sense of grief for the brokenness of the world and to intercede for people all around me. I'm determined to grow up!

One of the songs I wrote recently is called "The Mercy Seat of Christ." I think that God is saying to us as believers to come beyond the holy of holies, to press through the curtain and actually become the mercy seat of Christ to others.

It is not enough to be forgiven for our sins. It is not enough to stand around and worship. We are actually called to be the mercy seat to minister to people in the end times, when people will be lost and adrift and wonder what life is all about.

Recently *USA Today* did a survey that asked these questions: Do you believe in

God? If you do, what is the one question you would ask Him? Forty-seven percent of those who responded said, "I would ask Him, 'What is the purpose of my life?'"

So many people are lost and desperate, and as the waves get darker, they are going to wonder more and more, *What am I doing here? What is life all about?* It's an awesome time for Christians to become the mercy seat of Christ, not the judgment seat of Christ. God is calling us all to move beyond being the younger son or the older son in the parable of the prodigal son, to become the Father to the world.

Welcome Home

As I stand here in Your presence,

How my heart is overwhelmed

To be gazing at Your beauty,

Called to life in heaven's realm.

How can this sinful heart

Begin to grasp Your gift of grace?

King of kings,

Lord of lords,

Holy One who took my place.

It's Your mercy, oh Lord.

It's Your mercy alone.

It's Your mercy that welcomes

This child to Your throne.

It's Your mercy, oh Lord.

It's Your mercy alone.

It's Your mercy that says

To this child, "Come on home."

About the Author

Sheila Walsh is a powerful Christian communicator who is a unique combination of singer, songwriter, author, speaker, and television talk-show host. She is a featured speaker at the nationwide Women of Faith Conferences and has just released her new Celtic album, *Blue Waters*, with Integrity Music. Former cohost of *The 700 Club* and host of her own show, *Heart to Heart with Sheila Walsh*, on the Family Channel, she is the author of *Honestly* and *Life Is Tough But God Is Faithful.*

Sheila and her husband, Barry, and their son, Christian, live in Franklin, Tennessee.

For information on Sheila's tour schedule and her online bookstore, see her Web site at www.sheilawalsh.com.

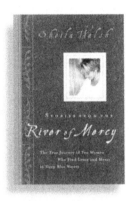

THE COMPANION TO THIS JOURNAL:
Stories from the River of Mercy
THE TRUE JOURNEY OF TWO WOMEN WHO
FIND GRACE AND MERCY IN DEEP BLUE WATERS

When Sheila Walsh met her mother-in-law, Eleanor, they stood on opposite sides of an invisible, and seemingly unsurmountable, wall. But when Eleanor was diagnosed with terminal liver cancer, everything changed. By God's grace and mercy, the wall between the two women came tumbling down as they faced deep blue waters together.

Stories from the River of Mercy is a poignant, sometimes humorous, and candid chronicle of two turning points in Sheila's life—the end of life, as she journeyed with her mother-in-law through cancer, and the beginning of life, as she experienced the birth of her son, Christian. Her simultaneous experiences of joy and sorrow gave Sheila insight into the precious gift of life and how we should live each day.

As you read these intimate stories of moments of joy in the midst of sorrow, you will come to appreciate the importance of life. Experience God's grace and mercy in your own life as you follow two women on a journey of faith through troubled waters.

0–7852–6875–8 • **Hardcover** • **160 pages**

LIFE IS TOUGH BUT GOD IS FAITHFUL

If God loves me, why did my child die?
If life is supposed to be so wonderful, why do I feel so bad?
If God hears my prayers, why am I still single?
If God is in control of the world, why is life so hard?

Sheila Walsh hears questions like these wherever she goes. In her own life journey, she has struggled with difficult questions—and found some answers. Not easy, pat answers, but real-life, lived-out-in-the-flesh answers that can help you find meaning and purpose in spite of pain and suffering. In *Life Is Tough But God Is Faithful*, Sheila looks at eight crucial turning points that can help you rediscover God's love and forgiveness. She offers encouraging insight into God's presence in the midst of our questions and struggles—and highlights positive choices you can make, no matter what your circumstances.

0–7852–6914–2 • Hardcover • 224 pages